Wommack's Life Lessons Learned

Reflections in a Mirror

2nd Edition

By

DAVID R. WOMMACK

Copyright © 2013 David R. Wommack Publishing

4250 4th Avenue, Suite 2

San Diego, California 92103

No part of this publication may be reproduced, stored in a retrieval system or transmitted in any form or by any means electronic, mechanical, photocopying, recording, scanning or otherwise, except as permitted under Sections 107 or 108 of the 1976 United States Copyright Act, without the prior written permission of the Publisher.

Manufactured in the United States of America.

ISBN–10: 1940357004

ISBN–13: 978-1-940357-00-3

DEDICATION

To Virginia—my lovely wife, inspiration, and partner in many adventures. She lights up my life.

To my wonderful parents—my father, Kenneth Wommack, and late mother, Mary Jean Wommack.

CONTENTS

- Chapter 1-Foreword 9
- Chapter 2-Values 10
  - The Love of a Wonderful Woman 10
  - Marriage 10
  - Family 14
  - Parents 15
  - Friends 16
  - Children 16
  - Age Coupled with Experience 19
  - Quality 20
  - Books 21
  - Color, Design, Composition 22
  - Professionalism 23
  - Dogs 24
  - Food and Eating 24
  - Great Weather 26
  - Old Clothes 26
- Chapter 3–Religion 28
  - Who's the Boss? 28
  - Overzealousness 29
- Chapter 4–Social 30
  - How to Talk 30
  - Looking for a Husband 32
  - Social Networking 34
  - Dangerous Stuff 35
  - Volunteering 35
  - Little People 36
  - Tattoos 37
- Chapter 5–Organization 39
  - To-Do Lists 39
  - Spiral Notebooks 43
  - Hanging Files 43
  - What To Do First? 44
- Chapter 6–Careers 45
  - Follow Your Passion 45
  - Working for Big vs. Small Companies 48
  - Strive for Diversity 49

References Matter 49
Mentors 50
Know the Jobs of Those You Supervise 51
What Are You Worth? 52
Sales 54
Chapter 7–Business 59
   Accounting 59
   Lawyers 61
   Multiple Bids 63
   Startups 65
   Hippo's Deli 65
   Underappreciated Auditors 70
   Hiring and Firing 70
   Fraud 71
   Minimize Your Maximum Loss 73
   Other People's Money (OPM) 75
   Apprenticeships 76
Chapter 8–Finances 78
   Personal 78
   Auditing 80
   Contracts? 81
   Where's My Discount? 81
   The Internal Revenue Service (IRS) 82
   Keep Your Overhead Low 83
   Confer on Most Purchases, Especially Large Ones 85
Chapter 9–Investing 88
   Your Stockbroker's Age 88
   Keep It Simple 88
   Commodities 89
Chapter 10–Farming 92
   Federal Hill Farm, Charles Town, West Virginia. 92
   Willowbrook Farm, Blairstown, New Jersey 93
Chapter 11–Travel 104
   Nature and Travel 104
   Adventure trips 105
   The United States Park Service's Senior Passport 109
   Travel Safely 109
   My Ideal Lifestyle 112
Chapter 12–Medical and Nutrition 114

Minimal Medication 114
The Joy of Coffee 115
End of Life 116
Chapter 13–Hobbies 118
   Photography 119
   Oil Painting 120
   Four Websites 121
Chapter 14–Art 124
Chapter 15–Growing Up 126
   Boy Scouts 126
   Summer Work 126
   Theft 126
   Schooling 127
   Auditing Courses 128
   Theses 129
   Social Fraternities 129
   Over-Socializing 130
Chapter 16–Retirement 132
   Retire before You Must 132
   What Will You Do? 134
   Volunteering 135
   Costume Jewelry 136
   Building Websites 136
Chapter 17–Recommendations 140
Chapter 18–Other Books by the author: 144

CHAPTER 1-FOREWORD

This book tries to encapsulate my life in lessons learned.

Learned sometimes through painful experience, sometimes through hard work.

I have sprinkled my own anecdotes throughout these lessons to make them more personal. I hope that at least a few will be useful to you, the reader, as you find your own path through this journey we call life.

Enjoy with my blessings

Sincerely, David R. Wommack

CHAPTER 2-VALUES

There are lots of things I value. Some big. Some small.

The Love of a Wonderful Woman

A marvelous feeling of endearment. That you love someone deeply—and in turn, that person loves you back so sincerely.

Virginia Wommack, my lovely wife, fulfills all those qualities that a loving and faithful wife should.

1st Corinthians, Chapter 13, Verses 4–7:

> *"Love is patient, love is kind. It does not envy, it does not boast, it is not proud. It is not rude, it is not self-seeking, it is not easily angered, it keeps no record of wrongs. Love does not delight in evil but rejoices with the truth. It always protects, always trusts, always hopes, always perseveres."*

And in return, *I love her so very much.* To the depths of my soul.

Marriage

Probably the most difficult part of anyone's life. Trying to live with another person.

My life has been relatively placid compared to many others. I have been fortunate to secure and keep the love of my life, my wife—Virginia Wommack. She, to her credit, has tolerated my usually benign quirks and eccentricities. My itch to travel, to change jobs around the 5-year mark. To change venues and cultures. East coast, Southeast Asia, West Coast.

Certainly Virginia has a better grasp of health issues. And I of financial issues. But we try to rely on the expertise of each other in these respective fields. Looking back, we don't always make the right choices, but life goes on and we recover, seeking the moderate path.

We don't agree all the time, but over the years have grown more alike in our response to religion, politics and living.

Health issues are creeping up now, and they will be dealt with as best we can. But we hope they won't prevent us from enjoying life and giving back in the continuation of our post-retirement years.

An Age Gap?

Generationally you *like* different music. You often *dislike* the other's music for the same reasons. That's also to be considered.

If the gap is great—say 15 to 20+ years—then one spouse will, probably, preside over the end of life of the other. Health issues. Alzheimer's. Home care. Home nursing care. A nursing home. Hospice. The whole works. Not a prospect to be undertaken lightly. Ten minute marriage vows don't convey the seriousness of such.

I don't come down one way or the other, but only reinforce the gravity of the undertaking.

Religion and Race Differences?

Not so much a problem—*if* you and your family, and your spouse's family, are flexible.

But some religions almost adamantly oppose cross-religion marriages. And if you live or plan to live nearby, those undercurrent biases and discriminations will grate severely. Ditto cross-racial marriages.

Beware.

Support, Don't Belittle

Constructive criticism, not destructive criticism. That's the ticket to happiness.

Each of you has different likes, dreams, needs. Be sensitive. A marriage is two persons. Not a dictatorship. Not one demanding, the other submissive.

Timing and the target of the criticism is quite important. If the "suggestion" always comes immediately after the wrong or offensive act, then you create the hair-trigger impression:

> *You tried. Failed in some way. Could have done better. I'm slamming you. Not the deed. You.*

It stings. It hurts. Occurring frequently, it dumbs down your spouse's initiative. Mentally cowers he or she.

Your spouse is allowed to make mistakes. Everyone does. Hopefully ones that can't be reversed. Those rightfully deserve decision collaboration.

Success Factors

The best forecaster of success in marriage?—Similar education levels.

Not necessarily exactly the same, but comparable education levels.

I saw this in an article thirty+ years ago and have found it to be true.

Other differences can be overcome, though a large generation gap and/or racial differences do present problems.

Don't Abuse or Raise the Voice

I grew up in a home, thankfully, like this. I never remember either my father or mother raising their voice to the other. I'm sure they had their arguments, but they didn't battle before the children. They must have done it in private. In a respectful manner.

And like the parents, the children. None of us have incorporated these negative traits into our marriages.

Physical abuse. Verbal abuse. It almost goes without saying. Get out of those marriages. Get away as fast as you can.

But the key is security. Being financially or otherwise dependent on your spouse puts you in a straitjacket. A virtual prison. Breaking out requires planning, effort. Separate bank accounts, familiarity with marriage finances, the ability to drive, a separated source of income, a mindset of wanting independence.

Thanks and Thank You's

Many marriages are devoid of these.

My wife and I hear—and use—those words often. Thank You. Thanks.

Every day is not too often. Nor several times a day, either.

Even in a marriage, nobody *must* do something for you. And when they do, a "Thanks" or "Thank You" is called for. A sign and symbol of courtesy. Of appreciation. Cementing—back and forth—a reciprocity of caring, sharing.

Little Things Spell Love

Beware the spouse or marriage that places a premium on expensive gifts and "toys."

The book *Men Are from Mars, Women Are from Venus*, by John Gray, definitely has some nuggets of wisdom. Foremost among them is the idea that women appreciate small signs of love. The kiss. The touch. The sincere thanks. A deep look in her eyes.

They appreciate them. Savor them. Cherish them in their heart. Creating a bond of love between a man and a woman.

Chores

A scheduled "To Do List." Same time every week.

Keeps me on track. Keeps my wife off my back.

It works. Try it.

Family

The ties that bind. The cement that builds character, strength of purpose, mutual respect, values.

My own family. Bookended by Mom and Dad. Who shared responsibility for our upbringing.

Never seen fighting. Mutually supportive. Discipline coupled with the freedom to make mistakes. Not get yelled at every time. Confident or hopeful that we would take their examples, make them part of our lives and personalities. Ready to pass those lessons along to a future generation.

Thanks Mom and Dad. Thanks for your direction and confidence in our ability to become responsible adults.

Parents

Mine were exemplary. Ken and Mary Jean Wommack.

Raised and coped with four kids. Three boys and a girl. Myself, Dick, Jane and Paul.

We never heard my parents fight, yell or scream at each other. I'm sure they had their spats, but they shielded us.

They tried their best to be impartial, not favoring any one of us.

Steered us to be honest, religious, compassionate, hard working.

Looking back I wonder how Mom did it. Raising us alone during the day, Dad at work as an engineer with Western Electric.

Too often kids are unappreciative of the time and money sacrifices of their parents.

It was a 25-year commitment to four babies, then infants, then youngsters, then teens—all racing to adulthood. How many thousands of diapers did Mom change, wash, reinstall? (Back then she had only cloth diapers, which required washing.)

I look back and think fondly of the quote of Michael Douglas regarding his father, Kirk Douglas:

> *"I don't mind looking in the mirror and seeing my father"*

It applies to both my parents. Not infallible. Yet they tried their best to properly raise us. *And all things considered, did a remarkable job.*

Friends

Neither Virginia nor I are partiers. Or big socializers. We enjoy each others' company and more often than not do things together.

Our true friends are few.

True friends?—Who or what are they?

Certainly Virginia is a true friend—and she and I have a few, in addition.

True friends back you up when you're feeling blue. Encourage and support you in your endeavors. Keep a steel-trap, closed-mouth if you pour out your troubles. *And tell you the truth.* They don't abandon you in times of emotional need.

Other friends you see often. Socialize with. Know their habits and foibles—But never reach the point of absolute two-way honesty.

We need friends and we need a few true friends. Life without them is empty. God and religion don't suffice, at least for me. It's the personal, one-on-one contact and encouragement that bucks you up, supports you psychologically. Another cares about you. You care about them.

Passion has its place, but friendship is lasting.

Children

Alternatives

OK for others. But Virginia and I decided early on *not* to have children.

Selfish? Yes. But with a caveat.

Virginia, to her immense credit, *was the sole supporter of her Filipino family*. Mother, father, plus *nine siblings*. Food, clothing, shelter. *Then she educated 15 of her siblings, nephews and nieces.* High school. College. All on the salary of a nurse in the 1970's. An "exchange nurse" in Philadelphia earning $130 per month plus room and board. Keeping $10 per month as spending money—and sending the rest home.

If that's not loyalty and sacrifice for family and duty, then nothing is. A huge gold star in Saint Peter's ledger.

Continuing through the 1980's and 1990's—and for several years after our 2000 retirement. Helping, educating. Testing our financial resources, once we were married. *But no regrets.*

We did adopt one. Virginia's niece, Emerald. She grew up in Catmon and we knew her during those years.

We started the adoption process when she was fourteen. Took three years to complete and get her to the USA. Just past her sixteenth birthday (before which it would have been much, much easier and quicker for her to achieve United States citizenship).

Put her in the eleventh grade at a Catholic high school in East Stroudsburg, Pennsylvania. In the Philippines she had already graduated from high school, but ten years was all that was required there. We were especially concerned that she complete another two years (12 total) of high school to catch up to her peers, improve her English and reading skills, mature, and acclimatize to the United States.

It was hard. Homework often required "Dad" to tutor. Often the tears flowed—"It's too hard."

But she survived.

So we had lots of "responsibilities"—other than having kids of our own.

Today too much emphasis is placed on having kids. Kids are often selfish interests of the parents.

Once started, each child ties you down for twenty years. Often longer. And returning to the nest is common now.

The earth long ago lost the need to propagate and populate. Per capita resources are shrinking, not expanding.

Children comfort, succor and support you in your old age?—That dictum is rapidly waning.

Kick 'Em Out of the House

We've seen this most visibly demonstrated among our circles of friends.

A propensity to hold the children too close. Close physically. Not encourage their independence. Their creativity.

Why not attend the community college in town, in the next town? So we can see you often, not miss you?

They hang onto the apron strings. Can never fly. You make all their big decisions.

The sad part? Too many parents, out of selfishness—in return for their children living, working, going to college nearby—let them freely make disastrous educational and career choices. The world is hyper-competitive now. Such lackadaisical attention to their future forecasts real, lasting trouble.

They then come back home. Dependent on you financially. Sometimes never righting the ship.

Brief sojourns at home are OK. But after a few months, asking "rent" makes sense. Freebies aren't appreciated. Leeches develop.

If you want to be proud, force them to be independent.

If you want pets, buy a dog.

Age Coupled with Experience

Too often we discriminate on the basis of age. Discriminate is not exactly the right word. We make assumptions based on age. We assume people are too old, out-of-date, past their prime—*before* we know their stories. Their histories. Before we understand their past accomplishments, their health problems, their still unmet dreams.

Ask questions. Get to know people. Make connections.

There are unsung heroes all around. Hiding in plain sight. In the apartment or house next to you. Around the block. In your department at work. They have jobs, histories, lives and contributions separate from their professions—generosity of heart, achievements, ideas, hopes.

But they won't open up *unless you ask*. They *want* to share their stories. You should *want* to learn them.

We depend on each other. That's the "Village."

You never know when they'll need your help or you'll need theirs. When a friend-of-a-friend can provide assistance, direction, ideas—or help—to someone else you know.

Connections enrich our lives. Make us better people. Seek them out.

Quality

Quality is a conundrum. Value must be considered too.

I appreciate quality. Of craftsmen. Of manufacturing. Of food and service. Not drink so much, as we definitely aren't serious drinkers or wine lovers.

Yet, as much as I can often recognize the years—sometimes a lifetime—that went into creating a quality piece, I have my needs. I need value. I don't have an unlimited budget. I can only fit so many "highest quality" items in it—or settle for lesser quality. I work on the cash plan. I save, then spend. And carefully.

I appreciate quality—for what it results in: pleasing design, longer life, less maintenance. Not for status. I'm not trying to impress. *I'm* impressed by true quality.

Nature presents an overpowering quality that man cannot approach. How far we still need to travel to meet God. Yet He presents his works of nature at our feet.

Quality people impress me too. But they come in all shapes and sizes. No parameters or molds can generalize. *You know them when you meet them:*

—A teacher who instills knowledge and a clear vision of a possible bright future.

—A Mexican laborer who works 18 hours a day and supports a family of eight.

—A nurse who gives her all for her patients, connecting both professionally and personally.

—A secretary, a single mother of two, who receives no help from the father, but who struggles to help with her children's homework and reading.

—A used-car salesman who busts his ass after work every day, coaching a little-league baseball team.

People who give as much or more than they have received.

Give to others. Not money. Time and energy.

Books

The world of books. They were a big part of our childhood and growth. Kingdoms of knowledge and adventure.

Reading

It began with Mom and Dad reading bedtime stories. The classics. Continuing in high school. As a part-time public library assistant (on weekends), I shelved books for a pittance. And read feverishly in the back room when the work slowed down.

Taking Evelyn Woods' *Reading Dynamics*, a well-respected speed-reading course/system. Helpful. Worth the bucks. Teaches you how to push your speed—although the long-term improvement is probably 2X to 3X. Not as high as touted.

Now I shun science fiction (to which I was addicted for about two years in high school) and low quality fiction. Non-fiction has more concrete benefits. *Biographies and autobiographies enthrall me.* Once in a while I'll re-read a few pages from the classic books. And still find myself amazed at the quality of their writing. Accolades well deserved. The cadence of great wordsmiths. Their dead-on choice of words and phrasing.

Where Is My Book?

Never be without one.

How often are you caught waiting. 5 minutes. 10 minutes. 15 minutes. 30 minutes. An hour.

What a waste.

Add them up over a lifetime and it's a colossal waste.

I've always have a book, magazine or reading material at hand. One of mine I can re-read. Poems. Non-fiction. Or from the public library (bless them—and from which I usually have six to ten books checked out simultaneously).

Color, Design, Composition

I learned this from several life experiences, not in a direct attack manner.

Composition—from my 45 years of photography.

Color and Design—from Murray Multimedia—a one-year stint, working as a multi-media salesman for this small advertising company in Blairstown, New Jersey. They did print ads, brochures and DVD's—with pharmaceutical companies often being their clients. While my efforts produced few results, I gained a keen appreciation for design and color.

Shadows, Tones, Color—from my oil painting and studying the art of those far more talented than I. In books, museums and galleries. It's not unusual for me, on an occasional pilgrimage back to New York City, to visit a dozen museums and 500 galleries.

Color—my painting taught me color mixing, which is an acquired talent.

What have I learned? Good composition and design come naturally now. I see the value of chiaroscuro (the play of dark and light, shadows). I see that portraits, figures, landscapes can tolerate radical color as long as the tones are true. That the choice of colors is critical to quality results. And that many modern artists (and older ones) present colors that are not pleasing. They clash. They "just don't work."

Professionalism

In our house on Elizabeth Avenue, in Winston-Salem, while growing up, at the corner of our 100-foot driveway stood a sweet gum tree. Probably 90 feet or higher. It was older and on closer inspection starting to decay internally. A safety risk, should it fall.

Bringing one of these down without a crashing disaster wouldn't be easy.

Bring on the pros.

They came. Surveyed the tree, the surrounding houses and landscape, shrubbery, fences.

"It will fall right here."

"You've got to be kidding. How can you say that so confidently?"

"Because I'm a pro."

Six inches. They laid that tree down a line that didn't deviate more than 6 inches from their planned path.

Never underestimate the professionalism and knowhow of the best. If your job is a doozy, they can deliver. The price may be high—but the alternatives may be lousy.

Dogs

Man's best friend. No question about it. Over the years we've had Dobermans, labs, German shepherds, Chihuahuas. Many rescue dogs.

They are miracle workers contributing to Virginia and my sanity and pleasure.

Ever giving. Demanding our attention. Giving more than we received. Adding to our home. Pulling us away from self-interests and *giving us unconditional love*.

When one spouse must be away for awhile, they provide a vital bond of friendship for the spouse left behind. Chasing away the blues and loneliness. A lifesaver, a sometimes marriage-saver.

They get old, pass on, bring tears when we have to let go. But no home that can care for them properly should be without one.

Food and Eating

I enjoy food. Who doesn't? My taste buds like to explore the cuisine of many cultures. Beyond my everyday pocketbook. Still, like everyone, I have my preferences: American, Mexican, Japanese sushi and sashimi, Thai, Vietnamese, Italian, some French and Chinese, seafood and cheese dishes.

I do try to eat healthy. Watching movies like *Supersize Me* put a big dent in my love affair with the all-American burger. Once in a while, now. I don't count calories, but I watch them. And try to keep portions moderate. My lovely wife Virginia, a registered nurse and delicious cook, greatly helps in the fight against obesity and poor nutrition. She is a hawk on our diet. And thankfully it's working. We splurge occasionally, yes, but on the whole are able to stick to it.

Movie popcorn. Ridiculously calorific and expensive. NG.

Sushi and sashimi. Once in awhile. From restaurants which do a brisk turnover and you can be assured of freshness.

Breaded portions and French fries. Mostly avoid.

While traveling, so many restaurant specials include fries. Best to try to substitute a salad and/or split one entrée with your spouse. Stay trim by halving the calories.

Grocery stores. We moved to San Diego under the dictum that we would only move to a place close to a Trader Joe's grocery. Healthy, fresh, much less expensive due to their private labeling. Friendly, helpful, knowledgeable employees. Can't recommend it highly enough.

At home. We cook simply.

For dinner: an entrée, salad, veggie. A square or two of dark chocolate for desert.

For lunch: a healthy snack.

For breakfast: a fruit smoothie or fresh fruit (sometimes with Virginia's homemade yogurt), and peanut butter and jelly on a half bagel (keeps your hunger down for hours).

Eating out. An entrée, coffee. Two entrees, if we must, shared.

Keep it simple. Fresh is good. Value quality. If you over-order, take some home. Your next meal.

Don't let calories, sodium, fat overtake you. Shun processed meats and buy organic if the price differential is reasonable. The lowest cost isn't always the best for you.

Great Weather

Four seasons are nice. I grew up with them in North Carolina and later working in New York and New Jersey. Snow and ice (not being skiers) created problems. But seeing, feeling the change of seasons, adds a refreshing kaleidoscope to life.

Our ten years of retirement in the Philippines was bereft of seasons. Hot and hotter. Humid and sweltering. I missed the four seasons, especially at Christmas-time.

San Diego offers a nice, moderate climate. Cooler in the winter, without snow and ice to vex us. Not too cool. Light jacket only. And summer? Not too hot either. Much hotter inland. Humidity—not a problem in a desert climate. And it's nice seeing others at the beach with skateboards, surfboards, wetsuits, shorts.

Old Clothes

Love 'em. Nothing feels as good.

Virginia jokes that I want to be buried with my L.L.Bean boots, jeans, my vest, my long-sleeved canvas shirts and wool hat— along with my M&M candies.

She's right.

Thankfully we now live in Hillcrest, San Diego, a particularly laid-back neighborhood. Every age, style and condition of clothes are worn here. Day or night. No one thinks twice about it.

I don't make a habit of going out dressed seedily, but around the house and occasionally out. No one cares.

Anyway, who am I trying to impress,?

WOMMACK'S LIFE LESSONS LEARNED

CHAPTER 3–RELIGION

Who's the Boss?

One day I was auditing a smaller Wall Street brokerage firm and had occasion to visit the accounts payable department. There I struck up a conversation with a large, black, accounts payable clerk. She came from the South and was brought up in the Baptist Church. And for some reason we started briefly discussing religion. How so many of the world's troubles seemed to revolve around religion. One religion thinks another's beliefs are heresy. It should be destroyed. Threatens them. Threatens their way of life. I couldn't but agree. But *her mantra* on religion struck me as a fitting motto for a pluralistic society.

"*Same boss, different department*"

We're all trying to serve God. In different ways. Who really knows if there's a heaven or hell? We "believe," but can we, as humans, really "know" the right way to worship God?

All of the major religions incorporate some form of the Golden Rule:

"*Do unto others as you would have them do unto you.*"

If we strive to acknowledge God and work to adhere to the Golden Rule, to make the world a better place for all, to have compassion for others less fortunate than ourselves, and be thankful for our blessings—then we fulfill our best.

Heaven or hell? They'll be there or not. They'll take care of themselves. We've done our best.

Overzealousness

I'm religious. My wife is Catholic and I'm Protestant. We both grew up in those religions. When we married I began attending the Catholic Church with her. Didn't feel pressure or a need to change my religion.

At home we don't argue about religion. She has her views. I have mine. We are each free to express them, but stay away from arguing. Over time we have begun to converge in our religious views.

Growing up, my parents were religious. Active participants—deacons, choir members. Occasionally teaching Sunday school classes, ensuring that we kids participated in youth group activities. They tithed 10% of their income (how they did it, I don't know, with four children). *But they didn't try to smother us* with religion. It wasn't our whole life. Family, school, work—were equally important. Balance.

I've seen instances in our friends' lives where they let religion consume them. Most of the family-time spent in church. Unbalanced. Overdone.

And what resulted? Whether caused by that or not, I don't know—the kids rebelled in their teenage years. Became wild, uncontrollable. Alcohol. Drugs. Teenage pregnancies. Runaways. Some rejecting religion entirely. Not good. NG for the kids. NG for the family.

CHAPTER 4–SOCIAL

How to Talk

Well, not exactly.

Accountants have a nerdish image. Bookish, not people oriented. Not always true, but more often true. Especially in my case.

That was yesterday.

Our ownership of Hippo's Deli occurred after I had spent eight years in auditing and six years in sales and marketing of computer systems. I knew how to talk to people—right?

Wrong.

Between 5 am and 7 am Hippo's customers were likely to be in the construction industry. After that hour they varied enormously across professions, sexes, ages and interests.

Relationships with your customers, as in any business, are extremely important.

If you can't make small talk.

If you can't remember their names, backgrounds and prior conversations.

If you aren't genuinely interested in them.

Then, coupled with a good product—you'll not win their friendship, loyalty, repeat business, or get them to recommend you to their friends. *That's a fact.*

Hippo's Deli taught me HOW. Through practice. A hundred times a day. Forgot the name? Ask again. And again. Cover by saying,

"I have a terrible head for names."

But concentrate. Write down notes about the person. ASAP.

Start the conversation with any appropriate comment that pops into your head.

"Cute dog. What breed is it. What's his/her name? I've got (or had) a dog. What's your name? My name is ____. Are you from around here? Lived her long?"

Mundane questions—or ones that play off current events, their activity, their children. It doesn't matter.

Any connection starts the ball rolling. But it's up to you to break the ice and find that connection.

I learned to come out of my accountant's "shell" and converse with customers. I didn't realize until later how much I changed in that respect. Now when I meet people I blurt out anything that comes to mind, just to strike up a conversation. And my humor has returned and grown exponentially.

Puns, quips, off-the-wall comments, jokes. All's game.

It's also amazing how many businesses can't immediately recognize *by name* their repeat customers, their best customers. Once a repeat customer is noted, you *must* make every effort to "connect" and remember his or her name. So basic. So necessary.

And the skill of remembering names can be learned. It just takes time, concentration and practice.

Looking for a Husband

The wrong places.

You're looking in the wrong places.

Bars, at work, the internet, Facebook.

Trouble. That's what you'll get. Unknowns. Alcoholics. Weirdoes. Mr. Goodbar. Question marks.

Look in the right places.

First. Picking a spouse at work or from the same profession? You're asking for a narrow, boring life. A one-track existence. You can do better.

Second. If you're religious or value religion, most churches and synagogues have social hours after services. Age-band meetings. Activities to participate in or volunteer for. No better place to find a soul-mate who shares your values.

Third. Go for culture. You meet a higher caliber person in the museum, the library, Starbucks, the cultural lecture.

Fourth. Volunteer. You don't have to commit to an eternity. A session. A few sessions. One project. You can bail out anytime. *Do some good and look for Mr. or Ms.Right.*

Fifth. Safety. Don't be in too much of a hurry for intimacy or to get married. The horror stories on both counts are legion.

Sixth. Time. I waited five years to spring the question. Too long. But when I did I was absolutely sure. And I've never regretted that decision.

Living together is better than dating, but not the same as marriage. Time together brings out the foibles, the habits and traits that grate and grind a marriage to its death.

Social Networking

Relationships—not pseudo-relationships built on fancy electronics, devices, gadgets. That's what's important.

Press the flesh.

Sales. Selling. Romance. Socializing. Making friends.

Nothing comes close to human, one-on-one interaction.

Electronics be damned. Facebook. Twitter. My apologies.

They have a *small* place. But bonds aren't well-built, reinforced, cemented in the new mediums.

Too impersonal.

For one, they require too much time and energy.

Billed as more effective, efficient, more personal—they are actually less.

Fewer "relationships," better cultivated, reap a fuller life.

Who hasn't seen a couple, married or not, sitting at a restaurant table—furiously working their iPhone, Blackberry, cell phone. Reading text messages. Checking email. Sending text messages. Sending emails. In. Out. All about. All about others. Not about the two of them sitting three feet from each other.

If those are your priorities, you've lost it.

"Social Networking" is here to stay. Nobody sees it going away, in an electronic sense.

But keep it low, in perspective.

Run your life as a caring, interactive human being—not an electronic robotic slave.

Dangerous Stuff

The world seems daily ever more dangerous. Drugs. Crime. Terrorism. Chemicals in the environment. Greedy, luring conmen or businessmen.

I take a middle of the road approach. Don't press my luck. Feet on the ground. And if possible, make a conscious effort to stay away from danger.

Volunteering

Why?

Why on earth do you want to give away your talents? Aren't they deserving of payment?

Maybe. Probably.

You worked a lifetime to build those skills and now you're giving them away? Who's nuts?

I am.

Our blessings come mostly from God. Happenstance. Or luck. Some from our own doing.

We have a moral obligation to pass on our wisdom. Help others in ways that they cannot help themselves.

Volunteering is one way to do that.

You select that path or organization that best serves others *and* your skills and interests.

Do it. Do it now. Do it for your soul and the betterment of humanity.

Little People

I watched my wife in Catmon, Cebu. We were walking 200 yards from her mother's house to the river. Just to see what it looked like, after all the years. Did it differ markedly from her childhood?

In the river, down below a 15-foot dirt cliff, were two women washing their clothes. The way women in underdeveloped countries have done for a thousand years. Because they don't have a washing machine, can't afford them.

A glint of recognition.

Virginia recognized her elementary school classmate. Washing her family's clothes. With several missing teeth.

Her classmate didn't see us, standing above, on the cliff top.

There was no shying away. Virginia called down to her. Greeted her. Reconnected with an old classmate—whom she could easily have just avoided.

"We're 'above them' now."

That's not Virginia. She doesn't cast off old friends or anyone whose economic status is now far different than ours. Ours by luck, hard work or the Grace of God.

She doesn't lord it over them, emphasize the differences, show off, brag. No. She approaches each with compassion and friendship.

Tattoos

Not a fan.

Why degrade your appearance with essentially irreversible decorations. Which in many instances aren't attractive in the first place.

Not always. But often. It seems that guys and girls, men and women, get tattoos trying to attract a lover. Opposites attract? No. Weirdness attracts weirdness. You get what you give.

Stay away from tattoos.

WOMMACK'S LIFE LESSONS LEARNED

CHAPTER 5–ORGANIZATION

To-Do Lists

Price Waterhouse & Co. That was their name when I was an auditor in the mid-1970's. PW&Co. for short. One of, if not *the* premier United States and international accounting and auditing firm. I started working for them after graduating from New York University in 1974 with an MBA degree in accounting. First as a junior auditor, then graduating to Senior Auditor. Worked in New York City, their offices being at first downtown at 60 Broad Street and later uptown at the Citicorp building in midtown (along with their world headquarters offices).

The audits I worked on ranged over eight industries. Here are some of the highlights, the breadth of experience I am particularly proud of:

CONSTRUCTION

Coalcon—it was trying to use World War II German technology to convert coal to burnable gas.

Chemico—a biggie, they owned chemical plants and were building a billion dollar ammonia generation plant in Algeria (later completed by Bechtel after the owners got pissed at Chemico). They also were building a large chemical plant about 1,000 miles from Moscow. Of the course it was only the PW&Co. managers who got to visit those big international sites. I, as a junior auditor, went to Alberta, Canada.

Olympic Towers—Owned by Aristotle Onassis, the Greek billionaire. A 60-floor building at 641 Fifth Avenue, off Madison Avenue. The first of its kind in New York: a combination retail space on the bottom floors, and luxury residential condominiums above the first seven floors. Done in Europe, but the first large project of such design in America. So there was some owner/financier trepidation. Worked fine. I audited the electrical, concrete and HVAC (heating, ventilation and air conditioning) subcontractors. Basically percentage of completion calculations, and cost plus.

MEDIA

Newsweek—I was the Senior Auditor on this job at their Madison Avenue headquarters. My first experience with publications and fulfillment accounting.

The Runner magazine

ENTERTAINMENT

Allied Artists Pictures Corporation—produced the films *Cabaret* (starring Liza Minnelli) and *The Man Who Would Be King* (starring Sean Connery and Michael Caine).

HOTELS

The Westbury Hotel on Madison Avenue in Manhattan. Trusthouse Forte, a British firm was buying it. They own and operate a wide range of hotels and eating establishments around the world.

SALES DEALERS

Caterpillar Tractor (an Angola distributorship, headquartered in Manhattan)

IBM's New York sales office on Third Avenue

SHIPPING

Victory Carriers—a shipping company also owned by Aristotle Onassis.

FINANCIAL

American Express Company

A Broker/Dealer (I can't remember the name). This is basically a stock brokerage firm.

Depository Trust Co—they hold billions of dollars of securities for many brokerage firms.

NON-PROFIT

Phipps Houses—New York City's oldest and largest not-for-profit developer/owner of housing for low and moderate income families.

Every audit starts with workpapers. These document the tests of the client company's financial books and records. The junior auditor prepares workpapers, does the "ticking and turning" (audit slang for examining the underlying documentation supporting his tests of financial transactions and internal controls: e.g., invoices, purchase orders, bank deposits, delivery receipts). He documents which of these he's examined, and any problems he notes in the audit workpapers. His senior, the Audit Supervisor, reviews his work and prepares a to-do list—basically a list of things to do: questions to follow up; more work to be performed, items to consider, problems with a specific test, adverse conclusions. At each higher level of audit management, that manager or partner adds his own set of to-dos. Each must be addressed (answered, researched, more work performed) by lower audit staff. All before the audit can be concluded and a formal audit opinion rendered.

So over a period of years, working as an auditor, the concept of preparing to-do lists became engrained in myself and all PW&Co. alumni.

Now I do it almost every day. I do it like this.

I make a hand-written list of to-do's. In an 8 ½ x 11 inch spiral, lined notebook. Each to-do numbered consecutively, leaving a space/line between each. When a to-do or task is completed, I just mark through it.

After a few days, when many to-do's are marked out and I've added several or many more, I just rewrite the currently "open" (yet-to-be-completed) to-do's on a new sheet of paper in the same spiral notebook. Then I toss the old list into the wastebasket.

Simple.

So what's the point? How does this to-do list help me?

Organization and focus.

First, these should be to-do's that I want to either accomplish in the short-term or not forget.

Second, the list should be supplemented with another: TODAY'S TO-DO'S. Things I want to accomplish today.

To-do lists keep me from forgetting what I need to accomplish. The TODAY list really forces me to both put down what I think I can accomplish—*and also do them.*

This single organization technique—making to-do lists—can dramatically improve your productivity.

Accomplish more. Focus on your priorities. Not lose track of the dozens of small to-do's. Everything in one place. Easy to scan for items that can be done in 15 minutes or an hour of time that you have now.

Spiral Notebooks

Ubiquitous. Costing about a dollar. Lined. 8 ½ x 11 inches (smaller if you must, though 8 ½ x 11 is the ideal size for filing).

So why use them?

First, they are easily carried around.

Second, they can keep all your daily notes in one place—covering anything you're doing: notes, results of phone calls, ideas, research, writings. At hand, quickly accessible and findable.

As you wish, transcribe your notes, etc. from the spiral notebook to their rightful place in your paper files or computer. Finished with a page? Tear it out. Toss it into the waste bin.

Make liberal use of pages. Feel free to start new pages for extended notes/topics, or when you know you want to file the page. Sometimes it makes more sense to tear out that page and put the entire page in your paper files.

I go through about half a dozen spiral notebooks a year. They are my friends, just like the to-do lists. They keep me organized.

Hanging Files

Pendaflex ™ files. Sometimes called hanging files. Get yourself a good file cabinet or hard plastic crate that has rails alongside to accept letter-sized hanging files. That's what you want. Test the crate or file cabinet first before buying—with a hanging file, to make sure it will work with yours. Some don't.

If you commonly need to sub-organize one hanging file, use manila file folders and labels. Don't be afraid to mark/write directly on these manila folders important notes: telephone contact information, addresses, names, discussion notes and dates, people spoken to, account numbers. That way you don't have to rummage through papers every time. It's always *on* the folder.

And reordering Pendaflex ™ files in your file drawer is simple.

Even in this high-tech, computerized electronic age, paper documents must be sorted, filed, kept. Relying too much on the computer is dangerous. Computers break, crash, get infected, get stolen. All your data and documents on there are gone.

And buy a fire-proof or fire-resistant smaller safe—for higher priority papers. Place the "cannot lose" papers in a bank lockbox.

What To Do First?

I confess.

I gravitate to doing the easiest things first. The quick ones.

Hard ones last.

I try to reverse it. Sometimes successful. By shutting my mind and saying I must do this first. Do it now. Do it today.

Focus, focus, focus.

Then it gets done.

CHAPTER 6–CAREERS

Follow Your Passion

A much ballyhooed cliché, but with a lot of truth.

Computers

I was intrigued..

After eight years the novelty of auditing had worn off and I was once again itchy to move to another realm. Computers captured my imagination.

CIT Financial's data entry computer systems were supplied by Four-Phase Systems.

On an audit visit to Boston in 1980, I stopped in a computer "hobby" store. Shown a personal computer (of unrecalled name) next to an Apple IIc computer running VisiCalc.

Blown away. Completely. Steve Jobs was a genius. The guts of his machine was a paradigm of order in the then electronic world of chaos. I was smitten.

So I struck up an acquaintance with the Sales Manager, George Condzal, and asked him for a job as a Senior Salesman. He agreed and I spent the next six years there. I learned to respect great salespeople and the role they play in American industry.

Four-Phase Systems concentrated on selling minicomputers for "heads down data entry" applications.

The Internal Revenue Service was a big customer. At that time the IRS's data entry operators keyed in all numbers from taxpayer returns.

I'll bore you a bit with technology.

Digital Equipment Corporation (DEC) was then a biggie in minicomputers. It used asynchronous communication between its terminals and the central computer (CPU). For a word processing application you could watch their terminal screen being written (refreshed)—taking maybe twenty seconds. Compare that to our speed. Instantaneous. We would demonstrate and close sales by placing 64 operators simultaneously on one computer—and they would all be keying in data at the rate of 17,000 keystrokes per hour. You couldn't even see their fingers, they were flying so fast. These were professional data entry operators who didn't need to even look at the keyboard. Nobody could compete with us.

To achieve this we had a proprietary computer architecture—which connected the terminal to its dedicated block of main CPU memory (RAM) via a coax cable. Very advanced and innovative.

Data entry was our specialty, and my primary New York City customers were Ketchum Communications (advertising) and the American Bible Society. Training was conducted in Cupertino, California and later in Scottsdale, Arizona, subsequent to Motorola's purchase of Four-Phase Systems. Our headquarters was in Cupertino and manufacturing near Scottsdale (4,000 people). Once, but only once, I made the sales honor roll and Virginia and I went to the annual sales extravaganza in Montego Bay, Jamaica. A big blowout for the best salesmen.

I loved the industry. The excitement of new products advancing technology in leaps and bounds.

I asked George Condzal for a sales job. He said YES.

A refreshing career change. On the road of life.

So beware.

If you don't really enjoy a business or industry, then you're unlikely to muster the energy to do it right. Customers can see through it. Investors and suppliers, ditto. Who are you fooling?

Go for the passion. With money secondary. At the end of my days I'd like to be able to reflect and think that I have no regrets. I did what I enjoyed (maybe even loved). Did it to the best of my ability. And don't need to apologize to anyone. I was honest, hardworking, fair, compassionate and generous with what I had. What more can be asked of life?

My Other Passions

I don't raise them to quite the level of passion. Merely sincere interests:

—Photography

—Oil painting

—Business startups, from a conceptual standpoint

—Writing

In life and especially retirement, you go through phases. Working hard on one project or hobby, sometimes for years, sometimes all your life. But you may tire of one. Become bored. Have achieved a level of expertise or craftsmanship that suits you. And want to move on, to explore different fields.

Life is cycles. They move with your mood, your finances, your health.

Sometimes it's time. Time to move on.

Sometimes it's time. Time to recognize your talent limitations. Time to redirect.

Working for Big vs. Small Companies

It's a maxim. Companies like to hire people with experience in bigger companies. Same industry. Big company.

So quickly—with the first job if you can, but certainly within the first few years—pick your industry. Try to get a job with the best company in the industry. Do your research. Ask others in that industry. Almost any job in the best company will be better and offer quicker advancement and experience. Better than small companies without quality reputations.

Do whatever it takes to get in. Camping on their doorstep is not too extreme *if* it gets you the job. Visit them every day. Work friends. Friends-of-friends.

Headhunters? OK, but you should *never* pay them. The only good ones are paid by the companies, not by you. Work with several. Each has "in's" and relationships with a few companies—usually different companies.

Big companies show you how industry leaders do it. Excellent training. Take that experience later to a small company.

Startups require a whole different set of skills. Sometimes experience with a big company is initially a hindrance. Because after so many years there you're oblivious to the huge amount of support you receive from staff functions. Marketing. Legal. Accounting. Distribution. Sales. Location scouting and analysis. In a startup all those tasks fall on you. It takes five times the work you were used to in a large company—to cover all these bases with almost no help.

A few companies are known to produce superb general managers. General Electric for one.

But all else aside, *having substantial experience at an industry-leading company is a huge, huge plus* for job hunters.

Strive for Diversity

Looking back on it, I saw an amazing variety of companies and industries during my auditing days. But after a few years I felt I was starting to get pigeon-holed into construction audits.

That's a NO, NO.

At least for me. I like variety. Specialization is good. Variety rings my bell.

References Matter

In job hunting, references matter—to you the job hunter. Here's how to do it right.

First, don't put them on your resume. Simply state at the bottom:

References available on request.

Why? Because you need to know approximately when a prospective employer may call your references.

Prior to his/her call to your references, you should call each reference and alert them. Common courtesy. Tell them that this is an important company in your search and you want the job.

When compiling your list of references:

—You can't prevent prospective employers from calling one of your prior employers. But if you left under less than stellar circumstances, be prepared in the interview to explain "your side" *ahead* of reference checking.

—Get permission from references to use their name as a reference.

—Ask a friend to call the reference (after a week) and gauge the quality. Listen in on, or record the conversation if you can, so you can hear it played back.

References should be genuine

In the best of all worlds your references should be *very* enthusiastic about your work, work ethics, productivity, skills, personality, ability to work with a team, ability to lead.

Lukewarm references are the kiss-of-death in this hyper-competitive job market. If you re-contact the reference and can't get them beyond lukewarm, drop them from the list.

References *must* be enthusiastic. Otherwise the employer will pass: NEXT prospective employee.

Mentors

   "Somebody up there likes me"

Don't deny the value of a good mentor relationship.

The ideal person is himself an up-and-comer. If you're lucky, you might be able to ride his or her coattails upward.

A good boss is a start. He/she likes you. You are outstandingly productive and amiable. Make him or her your mentor.

Bring your personnel, sales, production, marketing, distribution problems—plus your career hopes and dreams.

Don't just ask for advice. Bring solutions. Well thought out suggestions and ideas. Then absorb his/her comments and advice. Openly discuss your career aspirations and higher echelon personalities—in addition to the business problems at hand, the nets and bolts—so you flatter him/her. You are asking for their career help—and that flatters.

It's up to you to analyze the organization structure: Parked for life? Competent? Stars? Who will block you? Who is your competition as you aspire upward?

So spend considerable time schmoozing, working with, and consulting possible and receptive mentors.

Know the Jobs of Those You Supervise

The United States Army.

My first supervisory experience.

My first brush with managing technology. Technology I had no prior familiarity with, except in the Army classroom.

I took the classes. Passed the exams. Yet never felt "comfortable" with the subjects. Lack of repetition. Failure on my part to grab the "experts"—the ranking Army sergeants—and get truly educated. Repetition. Problem solving. A more nuanced appreciation of sergeants' experience and expertise would have proved invaluable.

I managed, in a distant sense, but if there had been an emergency, 2nd Lieutenant Wommack would have been found lacking.

Fort Hood, Texas. Company inspection day. My company did fall down. And some of it was my fault. On the battlefield, it could have spelled disaster.

Hippo's Deli.

My restaurant. Our restaurant.

I didn't know how to cook. So we hired a cook. He had the experience, the recipes, wasn't asking too much in salary. So he was hired. Trouble was, it is a very subtle blackmail opportunity. If he called in sick, we were in trouble. Big trouble. Sure, he showed us a lot, but if he was absent, it felt like a choke collar.

Ultimately I tried to quickly learn how to cook. But when we had to fire the real cook, my six-month stint as "cook" was an enormous strain.

We coped. Even did well. But the strain told on us all.

Trying to do everything, I learned fast. But made mistakes. Customers complained. We corrected. Most, but not all customers, returned.

What Are You Worth?

When I returned to the financial community in 1974, I chose to re-enter through the easiest route: Financial Consulting. Temporary jobs. I found work through temporary agencies in New York City. No benefits at all. But I had health insurance through my wife's work.

Easier entry. Easier to get a job. Minimal interviews. Easier entry into a particular company you "cotton to." And if they really like you, they'll offer you a full-time job. I had a few offers, but declined. I was doing too well in the "alternative" job market. Making too much money.

I started at the bottom, having been away eight years from it. So I let the agencies suggest a good re-entry hourly rate. They wanted a good rate since they received about 25% of my salary as their commission.

My first gig? Goldman Sachs. The Foreign Exchange Department, at 10 World Trade Center. The building was eventually a casualty of 9/11.

Typically my financial consulting assignments lasted for two to eight months, tops. After six months either the need or budget evaporates, or—management starts to question spending so much—whether the company could save by hiring a full-time employee, for much less.

One job followed another. Here's the rule. Gradually, with each new assignment, I added to my "consulting resume." My education and permanent work experience/background stayed the same.

Since I started at a low hourly rate, I wanted to "up it" as quickly as practical. Ever mindful that being "out of work" was the worst.

My employers were satisfied. I had very good references. So I took a very aggressive stance.

I employed maybe six recruiting agencies to get the broadest exposure and let them know well ahead of my job-end date. So they could be looking for the next assignment.

With almost every new assignment I asked them to bump up my hourly rate. Plus 10%. Plus 15%. Even plus 25%. Always pressing *without demanding*. Didn't get too uppity. Always willing to consider all opportunities. A new major company. New industry. New type of assignment. New area of the city.

Push. Don't be adamant. The recruiters want high hourly rates too. It's in their best interest as well as yours.

Don't be bashful. The recruiters are your salesmen.

If you don't think you're worth it, then nobody else will.

After seven years my hourly rate had increased from $12 per hour to $85 per hour. A rise of 600%.

Step-by-step. Push-by-push. Not being "difficult." Just asking.

Sales

Salesmen

George Condzal. My Sales Manager at Four-Phase Systems (later bought by Motorola and renamed Motorola Computer Systems). A fine salesman. A gentleman. Considerate. Hard working. An excellent sales strategist. Especially on large sales accounts.

He screwed up and so did I.

He hired me straight from CIT Financial. Me with eight years financial experience. Mature. Financially savvy. Needing less sales training and management than a junior salesman?

NO!

We both misjudged. I attended the weekly sales meetings. The training weeks at various Motorola locations around the country. Prospected for new customers. Attended to the old customers I was given.

I learned—but only one-fourth of what I could have. IF. A big IF. *If* I had stuck to George very closely. Learned at his feet. Socialized more. Consulted daily on strategy.

He was the expert and I didn't spend even one-fourth the time with him to learn. By osmosis. By example. From the pro.

If you find a pro. Stick to him/her like glue. Learn everything from them. Suck deep on the tit of knowledge.

Product vs. Personality

Why are sales made?

The salesman's product knowledge?

The company?

The product?

The financing?

What is the primary reason a buyer buys from you?

George Condzal had it figured out: 90%.

90% of the time a buyer buys because he or she *likes* the salesman. Personal connection.

Not because he's in love with the product, enamored with the company. But because he likes you. Trusts you. Believes that if something goes wrong after the sale, that you *can and will* fix it. Make it right. Protect his backside. Keep him from getting hurt politically.

I don't agree. Not with the theory. That's correct. But with the percentage.

I think the percentage changes with the company, the product, the culture of the buyer's appetite for risk.

But I do agree the percentage is high. Maybe 50% in most cases.

So a salesman really needs to devote that same percentage of time to building personal bonds.

Free Is Not Appreciated

It's a hard-learned fact. People value things with a price on them. And more often than not, with a high price.

Give it away?—They'll take it. Sit it on the shelf. To gather dust.

But brag? No.

They brag about *how much* they paid for it. *How big a discount* they negotiated.

Our throw-away culture values the absurdly priced over something just as good—or better—but which comes with a lower price tag.

Qualifying

Lead generation and qualification.

"Buyers are Liars"

The sales cycle is a roller coaster. Never more so than with big ticket, big accounts.

You work two to three years. The sale is close. Management changes. The economy changes. New competitors rise.

Suddenly the warm breeze blowing reverses. Becomes a cold, clammy wind from the opposite direction.

Years of preparation. Years of work. years of schmoozing.

GONE.

A great salesman is a wonder to behold. They earn their commissions (which quotas are indifferently raised, and commission rates cut, year after year).

Throughout the sales cycle buyers rarely tell salesmen the truth. Politics? Financial constraints? Product deficiencies?

He's afraid to tell the truth. All buyers want to be liked, don't want to offend, want to keep getting customer/prospect benefits: Basketball tickets. Skybox hockey seats. Free convention attendance. Smoozing with the salesman's company President.

Grown men. Buyers. Don't want to tell you the truth.

Your job is to discern, from their actions, the truth.

Effective management of the sales cycle demands the highest attention to confirming the truth. By actions. By alternative contacts. By industry and economic analysis. By whatever means and clues possible.

Sherlock Holmes, where are you?

Sales Prospects

At every step along the sales cycle, prospects—if genuine—must reflect your action with reciprocal action. Otherwise they are very likely blowing smoke up your ass.

They *must* do something that requires at least one of these:

—Effort
—Time
—Management approval
—Spending dollars

Positive signs. Meaning they are coming closer and closer to you.

Don't see the buyer doing this? Then don't forecast the sale. Don't count on the sale.

CHAPTER 7–BUSINESS

Accounting

The old saying:

"Accounting is the language of business"

Well, it's true. Anyone who aspires to really move up in the corporate business world, or owns and runs their own significant business, must understand accounting.

Early on, in the early 1970's, as a young graduate with a Bachelor's degree in management, I found myself in Singapore. Running Cosmos Color Labs. The company had twenty Chinese and one Swiss employee. Cosmos Color produced color separations for Singapore and Southeast Asia's printers.

What was their technology?

Most large-scale printing is done on offset presses. To print a color picture requires four films. One for each of the three primary colors—cyan (blue), yellow, and magenta (red)—plus black. Each film is made by scanning a small transparency or negative film and superimposing a fine dot-matrix. The resulting "screened" films are used to etch ("burn") metal plates that are then wrapped around the offset printing press rollers—which etched dots pick up the ink and deposit it on the paper. One pass for each of the four colors, printed on top of each other, properly registered/aligned, produces a vibrant color photo.

Well, my stint with Cosmos Color Labs lasted a year. I played General Manager—the top dog basically. This with practically no actual business experience! Our Swiss technician ran the quarter million dollar flat-bed scanner. My job covered sales, management and dealing with the "Gang of Five." Four Chinese and one Indian partner. They owned the firm.

Believe me, it was a hoot. I had an undergrad business degree, but *no management experience*. No industry experience. And to top it all, the first thing I discovered (they were hiding it from me) was that one of the Chinese partners was stealing. From the company. He had literally sold one of the firm's machines and pocketed the money.

My dealings were primarily with the Indian partner. At least he spoke good English.

What had I gotten myself into?

And the partners' outlook was this: if sales are increasing, then all should be well. Ignoring the fact that sales to customers who wouldn't pay were crazy sales. Their attitude: sell to these customers—because "we need the sales."

One year later we had accomplishments. New customers and better "quality" sales to customers who paid their bills.

But deep in my psyche I knew what I didn't know. Despite one or two undergrad accounting courses, I didn't *really* understand accounting.

And the old axiom was never truer. If you don't have an excellent grasp of financial and management accounting, the practice and issues, then you won't get far.

So to remedy my deficiency, I left Cosmos Color, and returned to New York. Enrolled at New York University. And a little over a year later, secured an MBA degree in Accounting.

Lacking the time, money, or ability to take several accounting courses, I recommend you do the next best thing. Buy beginning accounting books and workbooks. Study them hard. Ask for tutoring by your friendly neighborhood accountant.

Don't underestimate the critical need to know accounting!

Lawyers

They're valuable. They keep us out of legal trouble—mostly. They have their place.

But don't pull the trigger and call them at the first sign of a conflict.

Take our "neighbor" in Blairstown, New Jersey. Definitely not your "good neighbor." Always a thorn in our side. Making no end of trouble. Off and on. The wife mainly. Digging up our plants while we were away at work, and replanting them in her yard. Slashing our inexpensive nylon gazebo sitting on our front deck. Repeatedly picking raspberries on our property, in front of our noses, without asking permission. Putting up a "Our neighbor is a dog killer" sign in our shared driveway. Several of our small farm animals—geese—disappeared. You get the picture.

It all added up to a burning enmity on our part. But what to do?

Calling the town police didn't stop it. Didn't help much. They said they couldn't do anything without proof. No proof. But we knew.

Well we never really solved our problem while we lived there. We finally moved back to New York, the big city. But for other reasons. Tired of the farm's maintenance needs—and our aging. Following, I guess, my mother's maxim: "Nothing is forever. Either you move or they move. Either they die or you die."

But we did score once. Probably only cost them a few hundred dollars. But gave me satisfaction.

Our neighbor's wife, Carol, convinced her husband to hire a lawyer to harass us. He sent us a letter threatening legal action. Wanted to meet with our attorney on the matter. I was delighted to get his call. He was polite. Reiterated the letter. Stated that his client had a beef and wanted himself and my lawyer to speak, to settle the issue.

No way Hosea.

Now our neighbor wasn't rich. On the contrary, hiring a lawyer was probably busting his budget. I knew the lawyer was in all likelihood charging him by the hour. The dispute about a well-water access matter, wasn't huge as these things go, and I was very reluctant to hire a lawyer.

So how did I get his goat?

No legal action had actually been taken yet. I took it as a hollow threat.

At first the opposing lawyer was glad to talk. He probably thought he could, over the phone, either browbeat me, coerce or persuade me to do as our neighbor wanted.

My tactic was simple. Keep him talking. Run his meter.

Every 15 minutes he bills the client for another $50–$100. The longer I could keep him talking, the more he would bill my neighbor. Whether or not he made any progress convincing me.

I didn't bend. But I kept him talking and talking. Maybe for 45 minutes total. I told him I wasn't going to hire an attorney. I could speak for myself. Finally he recognized the futility and hung up. No legal action ever resulted. I guess he billed my neighbor. And probably never got paid. So he definitely wasn't in any hurry to spend more of his time (uncompensated) on this bozo's case. Finito.

And the moral? Hire a lawyer as a last resort. Talk down the opposing attorney. Do your own research. Keep his meter running for as long as you can. Let the opposition spend their nickels on lawyers.

Multiple Bids

Projects. Small jobs. You need a handyman, a small contractor?

There is a natural human instinct. To accept the first—or at most the second bid or price given. He seems nice, honest. I like him. He talks a good line. Seems professional.

So are sharks. Not everyone is honest or competent. But...

Time is important. How much time will it take to get three to five bids? Maybe too much time. His price seems reasonable. It will take me time to check this guy out, talk to other contractors. Days or a few weeks afterward to receive their quotes.

Do it like the pros.

Hold your horses. Take the time. Get 3–5 bids. Google customer reviews of each. Consider them carefully. Check their references. Decide.

The pros do this. They accept and plan the job for the delays in selecting contractors. And that allows them to get quality at a reasonable price.

Do the same and you won't regret it.

Startups

I'm probably not really qualified to write on this. But I'll do it anyway. Because I feel strongly about some aspects.

Startups are complicated beasts. The small ones—tiny businesses, mom and pop operations, entail quite a bit of paperwork, fees, filings, estimated taxes, complying with hiring regulations, ad infinitum. That's the simple businesses.

Now suppose you want to compete with the big boys. A complex internet business. A business in a highly regulated industry (which one isn't?)—securities, insurance, medical, those affecting ecology.

Gird you loins. Lock up your family. This will be war. If you're tackling a software-related business, best to read the book *High Stakes, No Prisoners: A Winner's Tale of Greed and Glory in the Internet Wars*, by Charles Ferguson—an excellent primer on the startup, to venture capital, to initial public offering roller coaster.

It's not pretty. It's nightmarish, tricky in the extreme. And the success or failure is entirely uncertain. It takes a lot of talent—especially salesmanship, proper management, energy, stamina, and financial resources—in order to go the distance.

Don't undertake it lightly. A gargantuan journey.

Hippo's Deli

One of the biggest mistakes of my life was, between professional jobs, buying and running a deli. Hippo's Deli in Mount Olive, New Jersey—on Route 46 not far from the main highway, U.S. Route 80.

Financially a mistake, but a learning experience in many ways.

I decided to try the restaurant business. Was snared by three guys who had started a deli in mid-New Jersey and wanted to sell. We invested about $70,000 and became Hippo's Deli owners.

The worst fourteen months of our married life. To say it sorely taxed our marriage would be an understatement.

The hours were murderous. An unbelievable grind. Open at 5 am. Close at 6 pm. Then an hour to clean up at the end of a brutal day.

Six days a week. 364 days a year. Totally consuming our time. No one trustable to cover if you needed a rest. No letup. No rest. No vacations.

But we survived and learned several important things during our 14-month tenure—before we came to our senses and found a buyer.

Normally we prepared both hot food and sandwiches for walk-in customers. Hoagies were our mainstay. Specialties were fresh home-cooked roast beef (we cooked one or two per day, supplied raw by Boar's Head ™); fresh roast beef, garlic, mozzarella hoagies; and 6-foot hoagies for football game watchers, etc. (for these we might have to come in Sunday morning. Just what Virginia, Vivian and I wanted to do with our Sunday).

All the help (2–4 people) were minimum wage—which succinctly describes their caliber too. Except for the cook (Jerry), whom we paid $7/hour. I coerced Vivian, Virginia's sister, into quitting her "temp" job in Manhattan and working full-time with us. Virginia and Emerald, our daughter, helped on the weekends.

We sold to another couple. Albeit at 50% of what we paid. I doubt if they were able to succeed either. We lost $35,000 on the transaction. Plus fourteen months of our lives. Nearly cost our marriage. The order from Virginia:

"It's either me or the deli!"

What did we learn?

1. We hated the restaurant industry.

Don't underestimate the grind of the restaurant, retail food business. Only those who grew up in it are prepared for the grueling hours. Nobody should go into this unless they've grown up in it and are used to the hours and "tricks".

2. **When it's all on the line, the family can come together to carry the day.**

We worked together as a team. Each doing different jobs, pitching in and rotating jobs on the fly. My daughter, sister-in-law and myself were full-time employees. Each learned to work the grill deftly. My wife, Virginia, assisted on the weekend, because she still was a full-time registered nurse in Manhattan.

3. Don't be fooled by a slick line.

"Why are you selling Hippo's?

Because that's our business. Startups. Then, after we get it running well, we sell it at a profit."

Dumb me. For believing that line. The overwhelming majority of business owners sell for one reason. They're losing money and can't see a way to turn it around.

4. The fickleness of customers.

Tuna salad. I changed the "build" recipe from only tuna, salt and pepper to adding relish. Much tastier. Yet sales slammed. Who'd have guessed? We reverted quickly to the old recipe.

5. Trust beyond the family circle is problematic.

We had to fire Jerry, the cook. Virginia caught him stealing sliced meat and cheese. He would slice it up in the early afternoon, wrap it and place it in the refrigerator and toward day's end transfer it, placing it under his coat—which he always brought. Easy then, covered by the coat, to snatch it from the counter on the way out. Sometimes he wore it for a few minutes inside the store in the summertime. It's cool in here, right? Its real purpose: to cover the stolen goods. I didn't confront him in the store. Called him at home and told him "his services were no longer needed". But he knew.

Later we found out he was also stealing from the cash register. When we turned our back or were out on a delivery. The owner can't be there all the time and he took advantage of that. Lord knows how much he stole.

Now I was the cook. In addition to serving the walk-in customers, I had to prepare for catering jobs of up to 200 people. Hot trays and/or cold cuts.

A small business owner can't be present all the time. He must trust someone. Best a spouse, his child or relative. But in any case, close controls on cash and theft need to be in place. Surveillance cameras over stock shelves and cash registers. Bank statements sent directly from the bank to the owner's mailbox (which only he can access). Separation of duties between handling cash and recording (two different employees). And employees always taking vacations. *Very basic internal controls.*

6. Experience in your future industry.

A requisite to success. Work for the best. Several years, if possible. Your "great new idea" to conquer the industry is probably not as time-dependent as you think. Experience will outweigh brashness almost every time.

7. Taxes and filings will kill you.

Not literally, but even as a CPA, the filings, deposits, deadlines and rules for payroll taxes, income and corporation franchise taxes, et al., are nightmarish and unforgiving (I can see how many business owners turn Republican because of the complexity).

Hire someone else you trust (preferably a big firm) to do them right and be responsible for interest and penalties if something falls through the cracks. Whatever dollars you save doing them yourself is not worth the hassle, time and risk of penalties for non-compliance. And in a tight economy, willful failure to pay some of these taxes can mean jail time.

8. Complaints and feedback.

Funny thing about the restaurant industry.

Your customers get a bad meal and will not return for one year, two years, three years, even five years. Meanwhile you've changed cooks or servers at least three times.

Doesn't matter. That's just the nature of the beast. *Second chances are a long, long time coming.*

And customers don't complain. A few do. *You should be grateful to those.* Most won't complain. They just take their business elsewhere. I recollect a study done years ago that analyzed customer satisfaction. It found that if a customer is satisfied, he or she tells five people. But, *a dissatisfied customer tells nine people.* So every complaint should be valued—in a sort of perverse way. Because only then can you learn about a problem and address it. Fix it, if necessary. So as a result I don't feel bad at all about giving my constructive criticism or suggestions to restaurant or other business owners and managers. *They should value feedback, however critical.* Most big businesses have systemic problems which hinder or make it nearly impossible to talk to a management person with the interest and authority necessary to fix a problem.

Underappreciated Auditors

Especially in the United States Government, they have been proven to generate five to ten times their cost in added savings. The Departments of Health, Education and Welfare (Medicare and Medicaid); Energy; the Internal Revenue Service. Who can argue with that?

Hiring and Firing

Talent in business. A vital resource. You have to grab it, pay well and manage it well to keep it.

And if you recognize that someone, after hiring, is not a good fit? Not competent? Not producing? Not getting along with others? *Fire him or her.*

Do it fast. Counsel them. And move on. The lingering bad apple produces a mound of resentment and dissatisfaction among other employees. Those have to carry the blame, burden and weight of incompetence of their cohorts. Nobody likes that. It stinks.

If, like Martha Stewart, you pay 25% more than the competition, you have an absolute right to hire and only retain the best people. We owned and managed Hippo's Deli. Ours was an industry noted for hiring low-wage people. OK. The caliber often isn't the best. And we quickly found references were worthless. Too easy to get a friend to act as a friendly reference. Can't trust them. So we were forced to fall back on expediency. *We hired quickly and fired the same way.* In that industry you can often tell within one to a few days if the new hire knows what to do, has an OK personality and has a good work ethic. Even if you fire them you gave them a chance, didn't you? What more can you offer.

You have to have good people and need to find them quickly.

If they don't work out, it's easier to fire them ASAP than wait. Longer-term employees are harder to fire. Psychologically and legally. A hassle that leaves a 360-degree bad taste.

Hire fast. Trust your gut. Fire quickly and cleanly as soon as it's not working out.

Fraud

There I was several years into the Directorship. Internal Audit Department at CIT Financial. 650 Madison Avenue, New York City. Reporting to the Vice-President of Finance and the Audit Committee of the Board of Directors.

Life was rolling along. My staff of 25 auditors kept busy. Lots of financial subsidiaries to audit. Plus four manufacturing companies:

> **RACO**—electrical outlet boxes and fixtures. South Bend, Indiana.
>
> **All-Steel**—office furniture. Aurora, Illinois.
>
> **Picker Corporation**—medical X-Ray and CAT scan equipment. Cleveland, Ohio.

DAVID R. WOMMACK

Gibson Greeting Cards—Cincinnati, Ohio.

I liked the manufacturing companies the best.

Then came the speed bump. I didn't see it. Didn't smell it. And I should have.

My background was public accounting and auditing. We typically perform audit tests on statistical samples of financial transactions:

Accounts receivable
Accounts payable
Cash receipts
Inventory

We note problems. Usually minor. And give an audit opinion:

"The financial statements present fairly … blah. blah. blah."

And on to the next client. The next accounting period. Life goes on.

This was different.

FRAUD.

The smells and small signs were there. But my nostrils weren't sniffing. Weren't expecting the unusual.

It was my job. But I hadn't seen a fraud before. Didn't pounce quickly. After all, weren't there more "interesting" audits to do and monitor?

Well, I got my tit caught in the wringer. The fraud came to light. Not from my audit and pressing, but through another vein.

Egg on my face. Royal egg on my face.

Financial transactions. Suspect the worst. And don't hesitate to throw the gauntlet at it. Investigate quickly and thoroughly. Prove it—squeaky clean—or expose it.

Fraud. It can ruin your day.

Minimize Your Maximum Loss

A financial strategy that Donald Trump and a host of others practically live off. Summarized by MBA courses. Smaller boys can play this way too.

I learned it the hard way. And it may not apply to every situation. But frequently, especially with startups by people without extensive experience in the business, it will save your ass.

Royal Tiger Group

Catchy name. Not bad at all. It was the business model that this "bright" MBA flubbed.

Anyone can do that. Not all business concepts, especially if new, are accurate, can work.

About the last year and a half of my working for Motorola, I made a huge financial bet that flopped.

Co-partnering with Don Rogers, we incorporated Royal Tiger Group and sublet 2,000 square feet of space in midtown-Manhattan.

Royal Tiger Group was a Value-added Reseller (a VAR) of Motorola Computer Systems. Nothing wrong with that. Some did well. But Royal Tiger Group wasn't a normal VAR. A normal VAR bought hardware from Motorola, added its own niche, proprietary software, then resold the hardware/software as a package to end-users. Then further supported them. In return, Motorola gave the VAR a hefty hardware discount.

Many software companies wished to be VARs. Wanted to pocket quantity hardware purchase discounts. But aren't big enough to order in quantity. A middleman? That was the idea. The business model was to be a Master VAR to work with smaller VARs. We would be the financially stronger party between Motorola Computer Systems and small VARs. Royal Tiger Group to be the in-between, offering smaller discounts to sub-VAR's. And additionally supply them with marketing expertise.

We bought two mini-computers, Unix-based, but never made a go of it.

What went wrong?

First, the concept, the business model, didn't fly. Concurrently Hewlett-Packard (HP) was trying to set up a few similar Master VAR's. but the sub-VARs were too weak. Software-wise, marketing-wise, financially—every-wise. Their Master VARs failed a year or two after Royal Tiger Group. Our sub-VARs were just too weak financially (we carried their credit) and too inexperienced in software design and marketing.

Second, even if the concept worked, it didn't work fast enough. Axiom ignored: It always takes three time your worst time estimate to "catch on" and turn profitable. We were undercapitalized. Running through $15,000 per month. At the end of ten months we folded. And my marriage almost with it. No, all our money didn't go south. But too much did.

We lost a lot of money and Virginia was not fully aware of our outgoing funds, so there was substantial recrimination.

Bad business model and major dollar loss.

I always suspected my boss at Motorola had a glimmer that his salaried/commissioned rep (me) was doing this, but he kept quiet out of respect and the off-chance it would succeed.

Was there a way to play this business model with a Min/Max strategy? NO. So without outside investors to shoulder the financial risk, we should have passed on this "great opportunity." I recommend you do the same.

Other People's Money (OPM)

With investments or projects, people invariably want to:

—Go faster.

—Have more control.

—Earn a bigger percentage of the profit.

Slow down. *Think*.

If it all goes south, what would you lose?

If it's such a great business idea, then you should be able to sell it to other investors. They should finance it. You have the idea. You're putting together the project/company/startup. Someone else should bear most of the financial risk.

Build the business using low advertising, high public relations, word-of-mouth, guerilla marketing, and earned equity. If it's so fantastic, it will gradually succeed. Especially if this is a new venture for you.

Spread your risk. Accept a modest percentage equity. See if the idea works—if you can manage the business, and if customers will buy the product.

Let someone else take the hard money risk. *You risk your time, talent and management expertise.* That's costly since you are foregoing other salaried opportunities.

Apprenticeships

The United States doesn't have very serious apprentice programs for specialized trades, crafts, jobs.

Europe does.

My Swiss technician at Cosmos Color Labs in Singapore had to be an apprentice for many years. In Switzerland and South Africa. He operated a $250,000 flat-bed film scanner for us. The core of our business. Without it and the technology we were dead meat. A very valuable and valued employee. Necessary for our survival.

One day I asked him about his early apprenticeship. How long was it? The answer: "about fifteen years."

Fifteen years! *Not fully qualified for 15 years!* Needing a more experienced craftsman to supervise him for fifteen years. Wow!

So I'm a fan of apprenticeships. It's too bad we don't offer them here. If only we in the United States could train that thoroughly through such programs.

But the opportunity in any company, to develop a quasi-apprenticeship program is there. A clearly defined track to craft excellence. To tech excellence. All it needs is a push.

CHAPTER 8–FINANCES

Personal

No Debt

Freedom. Freedom from debt. It's a wonderful feeling.

The opposite is also true.

Debt starts slowly, builds inexorably, becoming a choke collar. Occupying your dreams at night. Ruining your life. And when you can't pay on time? That's when the incessant dunning collection calls begin. Some even threatening.

Cash?

People still use it. Sure, credit cards are nice. Easy. But the month-end bill comes due and pay you must. And if you can't pay, *then the interest charges start to eat you alive.*

What to do?

First, never spend more on a credit card than you can pay off *immediately* (by the due date). To avoid interest and penalties.

Second, recognize that cash is king. It give you considerable power to negotiate lower prices.

Vacations?

You deserve them—*maybe*, but can't pay immediately? Don't go the credit route. Stay home. Stay local. Enjoy your municipal and state parks, lakes. *Our world of nature. Our national heritage.* Free in many cases. The wondrous out-of-doors.

Need a Car?

Talk to mechanics that work on a variety of cars. Which older ones do they recommend? Consider also cost and ease of maintenance, availability of parts, and mechanics who know how to work on this car.

Buy an older used car with a solid reputation for dependability and safety. Don't be afraid of a car ten-to-twenty years old. Purchase from a single owner, if possible. And absolutely have it inspected by your own trusted mechanic. Test drive it for a few days to a week. Insist on a one-to-two week warranty. Pay cash.

That car will probably pay for itself within a year. Of course you'll have higher maintenance costs than you would with a new car. But year after year you'll be effectively saving yourself 9 to 10 car payments per year.

Need a House?

Rent.

The recent financial meltdown of 2009 sharply altered our perception of the risks of home ownership. Over-extended buyers. Out of work. Going from two wage-earners in the family down to one. Losing their homes, their live savings, their "investment."

No longer are housing prices climbing in double-digit percentages every year. Nothing but risk is guaranteed to the homeowner now. Even the home mortgage deduction, once considered sacrosanct, is under real attack. All in an effort to cut the United States government's deficit and budget.

And depending on your locale, the real estate taxes come due in one or several big chunks. The same with homeowner's insurance. Failure to pay puts your entire home investment at risk.

Want a Second Vacation Home?

Forget it.

You just feel tied to going there every few weeks or several times a year. Otherwise you are not enjoying it. Instead, opt for flexibility. Rent a vacation condo for a week every year in a new, different place.

The result: No ownership headaches (opening/closing the house, maintenance costs, agent commission on buying/selling).

Clean. Simple. Easy.

Maybe the cost per day or week seems high, but it's *far better* in the long run.

Auditing

A forgotten necessity. The old Ronald Reagan quote (said regarding a nuclear arms treaty with Russia):

"Trust, but verify."

Your finances are largely in your hands and control. All financial transactions, contracts, papers requiring your signature. If a mistake is made, then you generally suffer.

The time to correct things is before you sign. As the cashier is scanning your purchases (second best is immediately after she/he totals it). *You must check it.* You remember a different price on the shelf? Ask for a price check and go with the clerk to verify. Even large chains make mistakes with pricing on the shelf not agreeing with the cash register database (in which case you are entitled to pay the shelf price, if lower).

Are you holding up the cashier's line? That's tough. You morally and legally deserve correct pricing. They are "out" of an advertised special item price? You are legally entitled to a "rain check"—a piece of paper saying you can buy that item for the special price at a later date.

Contracts?

Read them carefully. Understand them before you sign. Some can be amended—from minor to major changes, depending on the type of contract.

Asking for changes? Don't take the first no for an answer. Suggest their competition will be more flexible on that clause or clauses. No way you'll sign with them included. "Changing your mind" later—if you decide to allow them—is OK. A bit of show, posturing, a stiff spine—can pay big dividends.

When you do sign a contract, do sign or initial and date each page. That way you will always know if pages from one signing have been substituted. Tricky.

Where's My Discount?

I once had a job interview in New Jersey for a computer software sales position. I didn't get the job. But I got a financial tip that more than compensated for not getting the job. Here it is:

Every transaction you do with a non-chain store (and even an occasional chain store), ask for something "extra":

Can I get a 10% (or 5%) discount?

Can you do any better on the price?

Can I get a better price if I pay cash?

Can you throw in a free _____ (whatever)?

Often. Very frequently. The store owner or manager will do a mental calculation:

How much do I value this customer?

Is he/she a repeat customer?

Do I want to offend him/her?

Am I willing to lower my profit margin to get his/her business?

Will he/she "walk" to my competitor?

He knows that once you are out of the door, *the chances of your returning drop dramatically.* A lost sale means zero profit. Better a smaller profit than no profit. Better to keep a customer, not piss off the customer.

Managers and owners get these requests all the time from aggressive, price sensitive customers. Each situation is different. It's called haggling in the Jewish and Eastern cultures. And there it's done all the time *with almost every transaction.* We in the United States have long ago forgotten how.

You need to learn the art of haggling. It's a game. A game you often want to "play." One which will bring freebies, discounts, lower prices—and get you more for your money.

The Internal Revenue Service (IRS)

I guess I'm basically squeaky clean. Honest.

I don't hide income. Don't like to stretch my deductions too far.

I file on time. In fact, I (as an accountant) prepare my yearly tax returns well ahead of the mid-April deadline. Then I wait. About two weeks. To make sure I can sleep at night. To mull over the numbers and consider any other factors. What are the gray areas in which I'm "stretching?" Is the "stretch" worth the risk of an audit? Should I just omit those deductions? How much of a tax difference will it make?

And to make sure I'm "safe" I often accumulate and hold back a few hundred dollars of deductions out of the "stretchable" category and don't report them.

In the 1970's I had my first and only IRS audit. Triggered, I think, by my larger than normal charitable deductions. Those were no problem. I showed the agent my cancelled checks supporting and adding up to the total amount. OK.

Was the IRS agent satisfied with everything on my return?

"Yes."

OK. Well, now I have some other expenses that I "forgot" to deduct. And I pulled them out and presented the documentation for them. The result? That IRS audit resulted not in my paying more, but in the IRS *owing me* $400. They haven't bothered me since.

Keep Your Overhead Low

What is overhead?

An accounting term. Your recurring expenses. Somewhat non-discretionary in the short-run. Such as:

- Mortgage payments
- Rent
- School expenses for your children
- Communication

- Time payments for cars, televisions, appliances, furniture, etc.

If you're married, ask yourself:

If my job goes away. Or my wife's job. Can we survive on one income?

What if both jobs vanish? How long will our savings last?

Most two-earner couples never consider the abyss. Since 2009 that chasm is a reality for more and more families.

The time to prepare is now. By slashing overhead. Cutting frivolity. Unnecessary expenses. A few hundred, to $1,000, to thousands of dollars per month. Over time, get back the cushion against the improbable.

Make a list of all recurring expenses and spotlight where you can chop:

- Slash communication costs. Do you really need cell-phones with internet access? For every family member?

- Switch from home ownership to renting.

- Switch from buying new cars to buying used cars.

- A less expensive school for your children.

- Slow down eating outside.

- Find the cultural freebies (*retirees love freebies!*).

- Cycle (gives you exercise and saves money).

- Consolidate vehicle trips.

- Take vacations closer to home—urban and state parks.

- Cheaper hotels. Home exchanges.

- Chill on the local beach.

- Burgers and salad. Split meals (save calories).

- Basic cable TV. Forget the Premium plans with endlessly repeated B movies. Try Netflix movie downloads and DVD's (a great value).

- Fans, rather than A/C.

- Ceramic electric heater (move to the den or room of your choice in the evening). Don't heat the whole house.

- 3X per day $5 Starbucks bills? You can do without. Get used to instant coffee, filtered water. Save $20 per day or $7,000 per year (which requires $10,000–$12,000 income before taxes).

Confer on Most Purchases, Especially Large Ones

It's painful. To have to stand up to the scrutiny of your spouse. But often he or she offers a brake to your tempestuous locomotive.

> Do we really need it?
> Do we need it now?
> Can it wait a few months? A year?
> Should spending be contingent on something else happening first?
> OK, but this is your birthday (or Christmas) present, right?

Likewise blowouts, big parties to celebrate birthdays, anniversaries. *Not necessary.*

Downsize your egos, your expectations. Real love isn't about material presents and bashes. Cards, poems. Composed and made by you, convey your love in little physical ways that add up to big emotional highs. Handmade. By your hand. A whole better level of communication.

My wife and I confer on big purchases and many small ones. Avoids waste. Avoids buying presents the other doesn't need or want.

"Money saved is twice money earned."

CHAPTER 9–INVESTING

Your Stockbroker's Age

Never trust a stockbroker under the age of 60.

I've always had this tenet.

Back in my early professional career I had meager funds. Nosing around. Talking to various brokers. I inherently gravitated to those who had seen many stock market ups and downs—especially the Great Depression. Those who respected history and had first-hand connections with the companies they touted.

I didn't get rich. Invested in bankrupt New York railroad bonds. Companies so old I had never heard of them. They were in bankruptcy court. Managing the liquidation. And the broker had detailed analyses and valuations of all their assets. Which were primarily land, buildings, right-of-ways. He spoke weekly with the executives, attorneys—even knew the judge. Well, it took a couple of years. Didn't happen overnight. In the end I quadrupled my money. A healthy reward for patience and risk.

Keep It Simple

In the mid-2000 era the market had rebounded from 9/11 and was riding high. The United States was involved in two wars, had slashed taxes on the rich and passed a drug benefit—all without asking the American people to pay for any of it.

Enough politics.

Stock brokers and pension funds were stretching for ever higher returns. Short-term myopia was (and still is) rampant. An extra percentage point return? Let's switch. Let's invest.

I distinctly remember telephone and mail solicitations from Merrill Lynch pushing Collateralized Mortgage Obligations (CMO's). A little bit better yield. Backed by America's favorite high-quality mortgages, FHA insured. What could go wrong?

EVERYTHING.

But I never really considered them. *Too complex.*

I like simplicity. Old school. Auditor instinct. The more levels of complexity, the easier to hide problems, obscure the facts.

I never bit.

Keep it simple. Too many financial engineered products look good on paper, but depend on:

- Unverifiable (to the investor) underpinnings
- Questionably independent rating agencies
- The financial worthiness (in a meltdown) of counterparties.

Enough said.

Commodities

Speculation

Forget the stock market.

Forget investing.

Forget blackjack.

If you want your guts to roll every day? Live on the edge of insanity? Make manic/depressive seem like a speed bump?

Then play the commodities market.

You'll certainly be sorry.

I was not yet 21. Wet behind the ears. Still in college. On vacation with the family in Myrtle Beach, South Carolina. Speculating on potatoes and silver in the commodities market. Working with A.G. Edwards, the brokerage firm. (I called them to set up an account. No one asked my age.)

Lost about $2,300. I think Dad sensed it. I would make daily excuses to make a phone call (toll-free). But at the end of the summer, my net earnings didn't quite total. Dad said nothing.

Luckily I learned my lesson early. And never repeated it.

Long-Term Investment?

Maybe.

With long-term fundamentals on your side.

But the commodity markets are bait for the shark traders. Easy to manipulate.

The news is good. The price goes down??? The news goes one way. The price the other way???

The market doesn't need to be cornered, for the professional trader to control it temporarily. And don't think you, as a novice, outside the Chicago or New York trading "pits," can hope to sharp-shoot them.

CHAPTER 10–FARMING

Not for the faint of heart. A tough, unforgiving life. Much under-appreciated by most Americans.

I had two opportunities to participate, to a small extent.

Federal Hill Farm, Charles Town, West Virginia.

One summer, during my undergrad years, I spent the summer working on the farm of my fraternity brother, Ron Widmyer. It was psychologically worth its weight in gold.

The farm comprised about 3,000 acres (2,700 leased and 300 owned). It was a dairy farm with 140 Holstein milk cows—plus a few hogs, a few hundred Hereford beef cattle, and several hundred acres of corn.

My job? Plow 140 acres of corn, bring in the milk cows twice a day, milk them, help with the chores, put up hay—and at the end-of-day collapse into bed.

It was a wonderful experience. I'll forever remember it. The good treatment. The hard, hard work. Drinking raw milk at 36 degrees from the stainless steel milk vat after a day haying. Hour-after-hour atop a huge tractor, plowing between the corn rows. Stacking 10,000 hay bales ten feet high in the barn.

That experience engendered a lifelong respect for farmers and farm families.

Farmers are partly at the mercy of nature. These days many employ high-tech ways to come out ahead and make a profit. *But it's a heck of a gamble.* For there are years of losses—where you're eating into your capital. Droughts. Low prices—below your production costs.

The family farm:

Few endeavors build such strong, resourceful, independent children. Few as well cement the family together. Everybody works. Dozens of chores must be done. On time. Every day. And in many cases they can't afford hiring outside help. *They have to be done by someone in the family.*

Nothing is stronger than a farm family. *I am in awe of them*—the character they instill in children raised around and dependent on nature.

Willowbrook Farm, Blairstown, New Jersey.

My second chance to dip my toe into farm life.

Ours was 40.85 acres in the upper northwest corner of the state, 10 minutes from Pennsylvania. We bought it in 1983 and sold it 16 years later, in 1999.

Small by farm standards. Really couldn't be classified higher than a hobby farm.

For tax purposes we wanted to run it aiming for a profit. That reduced both our federal income taxes and our local real estate taxes (New Jersey generously allowed a farmland assessment—reducing our real estate taxes by 90%—on all but 1 acre of land plus the house. *Only* if we could generate at least $500 per year in farm income. Not too hard).

We chose to do that in two ways:

1.–By renting out our 20 acres of fields to a neighboring farmer.

He planted corn, soybeans or alfalfa (for hay). If he planted hay, we received 300 bales for our own use. To feed our horses.

2.–By raising and breeding miniature horses (minis).

We recognized that narrow specialization offered the best opportunity for profit. After investigating, we chose miniature horses over llamas. In part because we were afraid that the summer weather was too hot for llamas. So we wound up buying three registered mini's in Delaware from a breeder: one stud, Sir Lancelot; and two mares, Madame Butterfly and Okie Dokie. We gradually ramped up to a maximum of eight mini's, including Sweet Charity and Chocolate Sunrise. All registered with the American Miniature Horse Association and qualifying as 34-inches or less at the withers.

What did we get out of our 16 years on Willowbrook Farm?

An appreciation of the tough life of farmers. The risks they face and take. The joy of spring, nature, new babies. The enormous amount of work needed to run a farm—even a hobby farm.

Our greatest memories?

Delivering a Foal

From Madame Butterfly. Around 3:30 am, my normal time to rise and feed the animals prior to going to work in New York City. I visited the barn and noticed Madame Butterfly in labor. Standing with legs slightly spread and the foal's little head and feet poking out slightly. Gloved, I quickly grasped his feet and pulled it out. *A huge thrill.* Mom and son, doing well. But we always called the vet—just in case—to check that all was OK.

WOMMACK'S LIFE LESSONS LEARNED

Snow Mountain

After a huge 30-inch snowfall, our normal snowplow guy, with his pickup truck cum plow, couldn't cope. So we called for the big boy—a front-end loader. $150 later our 200-foot driveway was clear and he had deposited much of the snow from our parking area behind the house. In a 12-foot high pile. Completely obscuring our tackroom.

It took two months for that pile to melt.

The Silence

After a good snow. Hiking up back. Past our 15-acre field to about 15 acres of woods. A far clearing in the woods, covered in snow, ghostly silent. *Almost a religious experience.* So still. You could feel God.

Lightning Bugs

About each second week of July. For a few days. The path around our lake resembled a fairyland. Thousands of fireflies (lightning bugs) flickering in the late dusk, early evening. *Magical. Completely mesmerizing.* Not to be missed.

Manure

It doesn't stop. Those little (and big) buggers—our miniature horses and Arabian horse—just keep pumping it out. Doesn't smell as bad as humans.

In Kentucky they call it "the smell of money." Not so on Willowbrook Farm. Just the smell of work.

Once or twice a week, my job was to scoop it into a large Garden Cart and haul it to the middle of our back field. Then dump it (we didn't have a tractor and spreader, so were unable to effectively spread it over the fields). Scooping and dumping manure. An unwelcome, but necessary chore.

Our Lake

2 ½ acres with a nice path around it. A man-made lake. Next to a small trout stream. Big bass in the lake, along with crappie. Plus beavers that floated down from upstream. River otters. Massive snapping turtles. Herons. Kingfishers. Canadian geese. Swans. Raccoons. Muskrats. A host of nature's creatures. All unique. Lovely. A few ultimately pests and destructive (beaver and muskrats).

But what a high to walk around the lake, almost daily, breathing in the majesty.

Fence Building

Our front 5-acre field badly needed fencing. To contain the horses and llamas.

So we attacked.

We ordered a 40-foot trailer load of 300 fence posts and about 1200 boards—direct from the factory in Ohio. $5,000 worth.

Delivered on time. He drove the truck around the field dropping off posts and boards around the perimeter.

I cut a deal with our good neighbor, John Hauck. He owned a Kubota tractor which he magnanimously allowed me to borrow occasionally. Here was the deal. I bought him a post-hole auger and he used it on his tractor to drill our 300 holes. A good deal for us and he seemed satisfied too.

It took us about three weeks to set the poles in the holes with packed dirt and nail up the boards. Virginia and I did it all, bless her heart. Our technique? She held up each board and I nailed them—using a rented nail gun. Not quite as good as regular nails, but very fast. We put in about 10,000 nails in one weekend. Wow! Probably a half-mile of fencing done by ourselves. *A sense of real accomplishment.*

Antar

Virginia's Arabian horse.

Name suggested by our pizza man. A joy. Like a grandfather to our miniature horses. Weighed about 900 pounds. If he couldn't see one or more minis, he almost went crazy. Got extremely agitated, running up and down or stomping around his stall.

He was a smarty. Could unlock his own stall and those of the other mini's. No problem. It took a non-regular lock to "defeat" him.

Very lovable. Obeyed Virginia, but when I tried to ride him, he stalled—or would sidle sideways, not forward. Let's face it. *He liked the ladies.*

Geese

Ours were African geese.

We were "just off the boat," so to speak, with respect to farming. After two weeks as the new farm owners, I said "let's get some animals."

Animals? What kind? We don't know anything about farm animals.

So we played hooky from work one Tuesday. That day of the week was the animal auction in Hackettstown, New Jersey—20 minutes away. We arrived. Got our bidding paddle. And before Virginia knew it I'd bought four fuzzy critters. What are they?

African geese—actually goslings (little, baby geese). In the bottom of a cardboard box. Piacking.

What do we feed them?

Knowing farmers sitting next to us cast a twinkling eye and chuckle our way—and directed us to the feed store down the block. A short walk. After we begged them to "give us everything we need to take care of these guys," we walked out into the sunshine. Kept them first upstairs in the farmhouse (in the box), then soon moved them downstairs, surrounding them with chicken wire. Lots of mess.

One developed a genuine attachment to Virginia. Wouldn't travel unless she carried her. All considered Virginia their "mother."

And soon they fended for themselves outside, crapping everywhere. Had to be careful (it gets slick!).

Llamas

Had to have one.

Started with Paco.

Purchased from a local couple. He stayed outdoors except in the worst weather. Had access to a shelter. Played in the back field. Nibbling the crops or grass.

Funny facts about llamas. They are 35% more efficient than cows at utilizing feed. They're naturally housebroken (impossible with horses). In a field or fenced area they'll always do their "business" in the same place. You can take them in the house (not really recommended). Extremely careful and dainty, never hitting the furniture. From 300 yards away they can see you coming and will gallop to you, stopping abruptly, and kiss you. But also dangerous. If they become too attached to you, they see you as their "partner," try to "mount" you. 400 pounds can do considerable damage. You have to keep a watchful eye on them.

Paco died. The farmer had sprayed herbicide on the back field a few days before. Plus Paco had picked up, from the droppings of the white-tailed deer, a parasite that enters the brain and paralyzes the legs. Probably a combo of these. We found him one day. Down. Legs paralyzed. No hope.

Our second llama we named Coco.

From a private zoo. White and chocolate. Nine months old. Photos show him in our living room (twice). With a red scarf tied in a bow around his neck. Never broke anything. Threaded his way carefully among the furniture and breakables. Trouble was we got him too early. He imprinted us as his partner—and later would attempt to mount. Virginia and our neighbor, John, were both "attacked" on separate occasions. Both escaped, but Virginia, getting knocked down by a 400-lb. llama coming at her at 30 mph, suffered a shoulder injury. Bothered her off-and-on for many years.

Coco also met an untimely end. It was the dead of winter. A foot of snow on the ground and Coco was alternating going in and out of his shelter. Well, he slipped on the ice. His leg slid under and was trapped between the ice and the bottom fence board. A freak accident. But he couldn't free himself. When we found him in the morning the damage was already done. Legs frozen. Required the Blairstown Fire Department to move him to the barn. Three weeks later, after our near-constant care, massage, etc., still no progress. So we had to let him go. Such a nice animal.

If we had to do it all over again—I'd vote to raise llamas over miniature horses.

Miniature Horses

Their names: Sir Lancelot. Madame Butterfly. Okie Dokie. Sweet Charity. Chocolate Sunrise. And many more.

They are cute. A hoot to breed. Dug a pit for the mare. I held her. Virginia managed our stud, Sir Lancelot (27 inches high at the withers—where the mane joins the back). At work they called her the "horse pimp." We charged a $1,000 stud fee with guaranteed results (pregnancy). The foals (babies) were the cutest. 12 inches high. Running around within 1–2 hours. *Amazing!*

It was the most fun naming them and playing with the foals. Virginia often took off work to play.

We could fit three full-grown mini's in the back of our pickup truck, with its low camper top. Passersby gawked every time we parked for a restaurant meal.

In the end Virginia soured on raising them. Two successive mares died of complications from childbirth. Breached babies.

Dobermans

Had two. Raisin was the one I remember best.

So lovely. Clean. Attentive. One-owner dogs. Great for protection and companionship.

When they passed I "buried" them under a rock cairn in the back woods—because the ground was just too hard and rocky to dig a regular grave.

WOMMACK'S LIFE LESSONS LEARNED

Beavers

Incredible builders of dams (made of tree limbs and stones—almost impossible to pull apart). But their weakness is their knawing.

At our lake they were too fond of oak trees. A foot in diameter. Thirteen. All came down in the space of six weeks. An assault that couldn't be ignored or condoned. We called the New Jersey Department of Fish and Wildlife. Lots of No Help.

"Can't you do something?"

"Well, the water is high in your lake with the recent rains. Normally we would trap and release them elsewhere. But if we try to do that now they'll drown. So, no. we have to wait a few weeks until the high water recedes. And by way, you're not allowed to shoot or poison them."

Hmm. Legal remedies? None. Illegal? A .22-caliber rifle. No choice.

Case closed. Future trees protected. On to the next problem. A regrettable situation.

Snapping Turtles

They can easily chomp a large broomstick in two with one bite. Tough guys. Usually we never saw them. Then it happened. A sunny summer afternoon. Two large snappers. Each maybe 2 feet long and 1 ½-feet wide. Locked in a conjugal embrace, face to face. Very slowly rolling over and over mid-lake. *For three hours!* A most unusual sight.

Isn't love grand!

Swans.

They appeared one day about four years before we sold the farm, and twelve years after we bought it.

At first sighting we couldn't believe our eyes. They didn't stay too long. A few days at a time. Then on. Don't know where to. But they returned—sometimes after a few weeks.

Their beauty a wonder to behold. *Grace incarnate.* Never getting too close to us. Always a pair (they mate for life). An event to shout about each time they honored us with their presence.

Bushhogging

Lots of fun. Borrowing our neighbor's Kubota tractor with its bushhog attachment. Capable of wacking down 2-inch trees and clearing brush. Using it—along with pruning—a definite sense of making a difference in the landscape.

Could ride on the tractor for hours. Just had to keep clear of the bigger rocks. Know when to back off those.

Moving Day

April, 1983. Our move to the farm from a one-bedroom apartment in New York City.

Three inches of rain. A mess. And in comes our 20-foot moving van.

Stucko, in our yard. Had to call a heavy-duty tow truck to "unstuck" it. A $150 bill. Ugh.

CHAPTER 11–TRAVEL

Nature and Travel

Broadening, just as legend has it.

Sights never to be seen at home. An appreciation of the majesty of nature, architecture and cities. People of varied cultures. A plethora of distinctive foods. New tastes and smells. Many delicious. Some too exotic. Healthy, or heart-attack city. A passel of choices.

There is nothing to match travel for embedding great memories. Memories to last to life's end. When you can't walk, can't talk, can't see—memories hold the quality of life.

I am fortunate to have visited these National Parks, Monuments or Recreation Areas:

West Coast: Yosemite, Sequoia, Mount Rainier, Lassen Volcano, Mono Lake, Mount St. Helens, Redwood, Crater Lake, Olympic, Hoa Forest, Hells Canyon, Sequoia-Kings Canyon.

Western: Glacier, Yellowstone, Grand Teton, Zion, Brice Canyon, Grand Canyon, Glen Canyon, Lake Mead, Mesa Verde, Canyonlands, Petrified Forest.

Mid-West: Badlands, Mount Rushmore.

Eastern: Great Smoky Mountains, Shenandoah.

And these countries:

North America: Canada, Mexico.

Central America & the Caribbean: Panama, Jamaica.

Europe: Britain, Scotland, Wales, Ireland, Sweden, Denmark, Belgium, Netherlands, Germany, France, Spain, Italy, Portugal, Switzerland, Austria, Iceland.

Asia: Vietnam, Philippines, Singapore, Indonesia, Malaysia, China (Virginia) and Hong Kong, Thailand, South Korea.

Australia

Pacific: Guam (a United States protectorate).

Africa: Morocco, Gibraltar.

Adventure trips

I'm a big fan. Not for me the most adventuresome. Just adventure travel. Tamer. Safer.

North to Alaska

June, 1969: Graduation from Carnegie-Mellon University.

The day after. I began hitchhiking. With my backpack, west to Seattle, with a 2-day unintended layover in Butte, Montana (a Mayflower moving van left me there, then coincidentally picked me up again after 2 days, still going west). Then up through Whitehorse, British Columbia where I caught a fortuitous ride with Roger Bartlett from Demit, Texas. A rancher, then truck driver. He wanted to go to Alaska and work on the North Slope (they were starting to drill for oil). We teamed up for the entire summer.

Up the Alaskan Highway. Gravel, unpaved at that time, 1,100 miles. No serious breakdowns. He was driving a big-finned 1960s Chrysler, pulling a small trailer. First Anchorage, then Kenai, then Fairbanks. The North Slope wasn't hiring yet, so he took a night watchman job. I first signed on as a computer operator, but was fired after I pushed the wrong button and lost 2 weeks' worth of data. Onward. Another chance. As an electrical estimator. The owner taught me and I worked on jobs valued less than $100,000. Since I worked during the day and Roger at night, we coordinated our needs for the one car. Worked out extremely well.

Land of the midnight sun. Could read a newspaper at midnight, all night (with eye strain). Wild temperature changes. Could be 25 degrees in the early morning and 100 degrees at 2 pm. Ice on the bucket in the morning and sweltering in the afternoon. Lots of gold mine tailings outside Fairbanks.

Come August I told my boss that I had received a draft notice and must fly home. Actually, having taken Army ROTC in college, I knew I had to report to Basic Training. A little fib.

Bicycling Cross-Country

While stationed at Fort Hood, Texas I took a 2-week vacation. Planned a bicycling trip from there to Winston-Salem, North Carolina, my home.

Bought a good bike for $140. Trained for 2 weeks, then set out. I had never really ridden much before.

Lasted a little more than a week.

Best pace: 93 miles in one day. Never so tired in my life. I lay down without padding on a solid concrete driveway and was asleep in two seconds.

Extremely strenuous. Moderate hills were OK, but Arkansas' flat country was the worst. No letup. No changeup.

WOMMACK'S LIFE LESSONS LEARNED

Tasting the Far East

My R&R's (Rest and Recuperation) from the war in Vietnam.

Every six months soldiers were allowed a 7-day vacation. I chose Bangkok, Thailand first. Sydney, Australia the second time.

Loved both.

Recollections:

Bangkok—temples, first class hotel serving Kobe steak for $1.75 (now it would be $100 plus), beautiful ladies.

Sydney—Bondi Beach, where the 2-foot waves are so strong they knock you off your feet. Beaches to die for. Best in the world. Red tile roofs everywhere.

Made up my mind to return to the Far East to look for work.

Hitchhiking Europe

Two months. Wish it had been longer, but $400 only lasts so long.

Marvelous time. Sleeping in youth hostels (they allowed older people too).

Caught many rides on the road and some by linking up at the hostel with other driving travelers.

Highlights from my memory:

Met a Dane who stopped to help us with our car's electrical problem. He literally pulled some wires from under his dashboard, cut them and connected them under the dash in our car to get us started. Then invited us to his 12th floor walkup apartment for the night (we were about four in the car). No bathroom. He/we peed in the sink. To defecate one had to walk down to the ground-floor bathroom. Wow.

Fabulous London. Attended the theatre three times a day for several days. Saw Sir Robert Morley on the stage, in *The Mousetrap*. Plays were ultra-cheap, in part because they play forever. Paid $3+ for each. Super time.

Slept in a chalet in Switzerland across from the famous Eiger mountain. That's where, at that time, only 26 people had ever climbed the Eiger—and dozens had died. Six thousand feet nearly straight up. With binoculars we could see the climbers by day and their lights at night. Crazy.

Across Europe by EuroRail train. Great time. If the distance was long, I'd sleep overnight on the train and wake in the morning at my destination. Comfortable. Efficient.

Stayed many times in pensiones with bed and 1–2 meals. The one in Florence was especially nice. Terrific food. Mama mia!

Used Frommer's Europe on $5 per day. Now it would be $100 per day at least.

Drank wine for the first time in Paris. The reason? It was cheaper than soda. And this after three non-drinking years in a fraternity!

The ferry ride from Copenhagen, Denmark to Malmo, Sweden. Got so hungry I had to have something. Ate an appetizer in the dining room—creamed herring. The only thing I could afford. Similarly in London, the cheapest item on the menu at an Indian restaurant was liver dumpling. Little did I know it was one huge dumpling, the size of a softball. I ate it, but it stayed like a lead weight in my stomach for a two days.

Slept one night in a cow pasture and in the morning awoke to their mooing, ten feet away. Lucky they didn't step on me. I didn't have a tent. This was Germany. Just rolled myself in a waterproof wrap and slept on the ground.

The United States Park Service's Senior Passport

The biggest bargain in the world.!

What you've been paying federal income taxes these many years for. Free access for you and your spouse to all United States National Parks (there are 58) and National Monuments (there are 100. National Monuments aren't just stone pillars with writing on them. In many, many cases they are really parks. Small and larger).

And what is the cost of this wonderful document, the Senior Passport?

Just $10.

Can be used by you and your spouse together. Good for a lifetime. AMAZING!!

Travel Safely

Can't be emphasized too much.

Pose this question first: How safe is it?

Crime. Petty. Serious. Kidnappings. Gangs.

What's the safer mode of transport?

Should I avoid that area altogether?

Meet somewhere safer?

Travel somewhere else?

Bring a friend or friends who know the area, the route.

Pay a little more. Be safe.

Hitchhiking

I hitchhiked from Pittsburgh, Pennsylvania to Fairbanks, Alaska in the summer of 1969. Rode with truckers and others. Only one problem occurred, which I finessed. The driver of a passenger car put his hand on my knee.

A friendly guy?

Too friendly.

Time to exit. I did.

These days I don't advise hitchhiking in America. Too risky.

I hitchhiked through Western Europe in the summer of 1971. A backpack, tent, and $400 in my pocket. That wouldn't buy a week now. Stayed in youth hostels, pensiones, and occasionally slept on trains. Caught rides at youth hostels or on the road. Western Europe is still relatively safe.

By Bus and Train

1972 I traveled the island of Java, Indonesia. Researching joint ventures (cigars, orchids, and tropical fish for Indonesia Research & Development Co.). Traveled by train and bus. Kept my bag firmly attached to me. A money belt under my clothes. And never ate raw foods other than fruit.

Only had my bag stolen once—when I forgot and placed it in the overhead bin—and dozed off. Poor me.

Never got the runs, though.

The Philippines

It's dangerous.

WOMMACK'S LIFE LESSONS LEARNED

Certain areas are notorious. Rare. But very bad news if it does happen.

Any Caucasian stands out. Word travels fast to the bad guys. Around the corner, around the curve in the road, life threatening people lurk. So we avoided those areas. Stuck to safer ground. Always went with friends knowledgeable about the area. And my wife still had to talk us out of some sticky situations.

We were at the Visayan Electric Company in Cebu City, questioning our bill. We patiently took a number and waited 45 minutes. Our number called. Sat down in front of the customer service representative. From behind us a man reached between us and placed a bill and sheaf of papers in front of the service rep and ahead of mine. The message was clear. He wanted to be waited on before us. He had no number.

I reached for his papers, picked them up, placed them to the side and said, "We were first."

He scowled, took his papers and retreated.

We finished our business and went to the exit. He stopped us. Speaking in Cebuano, he told my wife we had "embarrassed him."

"Why don't you Americans go home. The next time you come, he might be dead."

And with that he pointed his hand and fingers like a gun at me—and pulled the trigger.

We left, but pointedly never returned to that office.

In the Philippines you can hire a "hit man" for $50. Max.

Cebu City. Virginia turned our Toyota from the road into the entrance to an Italian restaurant. Made the turn signal but a motorcyclist, failing to slow down—though he had plenty of time—came between us and the entrance. A slight accident. His cycle tipped over. Not really damaged. He, unhurt. Only his ego bruised.

He called a policeman and took several cell phone pictures of our car and its license plate. The policeman was unsympathetic to the motorcyclist.

"Nothing broken? Not hurt? Then, *what's your problem?*"

My wife demanded he erase the pictures. He said he had, but she doubted.

We heightened our vigilance and actually discussed selling the car. *Nothing happened. But it could have.* Broadcast the pictures to buddies (gang members?) and they could be on the lookout to exact revenge.

Value safety.

My Ideal Lifestyle

A permanent semi-itinerant. Traveling, yes. But *living* in various parts of the world.

Spending one to five years in each locale. Adopting new friends. Soaking up the culture. Exploring nature. Exploring the cuisine. Flexing the brain.

Then moving on.

That would be the life!

CHAPTER 12–MEDICAL AND NUTRITION

Minimal Medication

Overmedication.

Now we're bombarded on TV, in print, by Big Pharm ads. Can't leave it to the experts, the doctors. No. they must stain the minds of the least knowledgeable. Soak up ad dollars better spent on research or helping people.

How many friends are taking 8–10 meds daily? Drug interactions? Cross contamination? Nobody tests more than two. So—we have no idea about 3, 4, 5, 6, 7, 8, 9, 10 together. *No idea.*

We're killing ourselves. Degrading—often unseen and often unfelt—our kidneys, livers, vital organs. Until it's too late. And we croak.

Kidney failure. Heart failure. Liver failure. *We do it to ourselves.*

Camigan, Philippines.

We were visiting a friend with our cardiologist friend, Dr. Tino Froilan.

Oh, why don't we visit his [Dr. Froilan's] longtime friend?

OK.

We arrived to find his friend in a wheelchair. Looking like death was around the corner. Taking a plethora of medicine. All prescribed by his doctor.

We were shocked.

Dr. Froilan to the rescue. His verdict?

Overmedication.

Now ordered drastically slashed.

Two months later: Up and about. Walking. Talking. Like his old self. A new lease on life.

Souderton, Pennsylvania

Virginia's foster mom, Catherine Landis. Feeling old age. Worse and worse. Feeling lousy. Taking a pile of pills.

Riding home. Listening to the radio. A news article about how doctors "earn" vacations by prescribing drugs. Racking up points toward their vacations with each prescription.

Catherine never realized that.

Shocked. Disgusted.

She took matters in to her own hands. Flushed all her medicine down the toilet. Two weeks later?

Never felt better in her life.

The Joy of Coffee

Forget hot tea.

Coffee clears the mind's cobwebs for me. Focuses. Makes me more productive.

It can certainly be overdone. Jitters. Shakes. After too many cups.

But in moderation. A few cups a day. Brightens the persona and your outlook.

End of Life

Nursing Homes

We age. Our health declines. Then fails. One spouse eventually must care for the other. Whether personally, in the home, or by placing the other in a nursing home.

But there is an alternative.

Virginia and I are lucky. Having lived overseas, we're comfortable moving back at some point—before our savings are decimated by end-of-life care. To enjoy 24x7 nursing care at very, very affordable rates. $1/20^{th}$ that of American nursing costs. With good doctors and decent hospitals.

A last resort? Yes. But financially prudent.

The Choice To End Your Own Life

Illegal in most states. Legal in a few: Oregon, Washington and Montana.

I concur with the minority.

We should be able to end our own life without legal problems.

Life can become unbearable. Health problems in the extreme. Pain. Suffering. For what?

What are we afraid of? Heaven or Hell?

What are we living for? Our children and friends to see us in a near vegetative state? In agony? With no cognizance of our surroundings?

I don't think so.

At our option, quality of life should prevail over merely extended life.

So we have two basic choices:

Go west—to Oregon, Washington, or Montana, or

Go east—to Belgium, Luxembourg, the Netherlands, or Switzerland.

Where are civilization, the rights of the individual, and compassion when you *really* need them?

CHAPTER 13–HOBBIES

I like hobbies. *I like serious hobbies.* Two or three to add balance and zest to life.

Your 8-to-5 work? Necessary. To pay the rent, the mortgage. To feed and clothe yourself and your family. But spare time, beyond your family? Your spare time?

Some people fill that time with frivolity. As a couch potato, sports fan, or some such nonsense.

I don't agree.

That only fills the time. *It doesn't add value to life.*

Is that the legacy you want to leave your children? The world? As people face longer retirements, is that how you want to fill it? 20–30 years of trivia?

Why not do something serious?

That's right. Trivia, nonsense, ultimately of zero value.

Who are you helping? What will your legacy be? When your obit is written, will your accomplishments stop with the day you retire?

It's proven that hobbies stimulate the mind. You'll live longer.

My hobbies started in high school, changed and added to over the years. And have immeasurably enriched me.

WOMMACK'S LIFE LESSONS LEARNED

Photography

A wonderful way to learn to "see" the world. See it through your creative lens. Tell the story the way *you* see it, the way *you* want it told.

A young classmate and an older pro photographer taught me. Very generously.

The pro, Walter Murphy, allowed me to use his darkroom. And coached me.

I did the photographs for my high school yearbook. Got permission and funding, then built a darkroom at R.J. Reynolds High School in Winston-Salem. And took the formal senior prom photos too.

My talent blossomed further when in college. I spent two weeks at a photography workshop. Upstate New York. Lived in an old farmhouse. Attended classes. Went on photo assignments. And used their pro darkrooms, dryers in a converted barn. I still have photos from that time. A drunk with gross abdominal surgical scars, grinning from ear-to-ear, holding a bouquet of flowers, his schlong hanging out. Not your typical Sunday afternoon stroller!

Buying my first Nikon SLR, reselling it in London for twice what I paid. Another Nikon bought in New York. Then much fun photographing our National Parks, getting the photos printed by the Time-Life Labs (the same labs which print the magazine photos). Photographing ordinary people in New York City—Halloween masks in Greenwich Village; undercover in a Chinatown siopao coffee shop; nuns bicycling in Columbus Circle.

Oil Painting

Two years into our "retirement" in Cebu, Philippines, I grew bored. Unable to travel to other islands extensively—for security reasons. Quite bored.

Virginia suggested I try an art course. Drawing. The Cebu Academy of Art had classes. A group of a dozen moderately talented artists. Teaching out of a donated space.

Could I draw, prior to that? No way. It was probably hopeless.

I took the course. I was OK. Nothing great. No Leonardo. But something to do.

What's next? My next art course?

Well, here were the choices:

Pastel—I just didn't like the results, the look.

Watercolor—you can't really cover up or correct mistakes.

Oils—you can endlessly revise and correct. And if I ever got any good at it, oils fetch the most dollars.

Oil painting it was. And course by course, painting by painting, I got better. *Dramatically better.* Often, with each new canvas finished, I'd look at it and say, "Wow! I did that? Amazing!"

One of my teachers was Luther Galicano, the nephew of Romulo Galicano, the foremost Filipino portraitist. Romulo lives in Manila and won the Portrait Society of America's 2005 International Grand Prize—for his life-sized oil portrait of a Chinese businessman. In a country where the minimum wage is $1/10^{th}$ to $1/20^{th}$ of that in the United States, he still commands $80,000 for a full-length portrait. And is booked for years ahead.

Eight years later, when I left the Philippines, I was pretty good. Probably only two or three in Cebu (the second largest city in the Philippines) were better. So it was gratifying, and with pride that I look back on my development as a serious painter. I brought 30 paintings with us to San Diego and sent 75 to North Carolina (where in short order, by personal salesmanship, I found three art galleries in Winston-Salem to show my work).

I also dabbled with excellent results in Japanese Zen calligraphy. What got me started? An art gallery in Soho, New York City. Selling a beautiful one-Zen-character on handmade rice paper—for $1,500!

I can do that! At least make a good try.

So I bought materials in Cebu, found a supplier of handmade paper, experimented. Didn't like Chinese ink (not black enough). Found that automotive acrylic paint was just right. Black, half combined with red, green, or purple—they created a gorgeous effect. But flat. So I created depth under the characters by applying 2–4 layers of a random sprinkling of very diluted Chinese inks. Darker with each new layer. Then, needing a source of great looking characters, plus meanings that resonated, I found a book on Zen calligraphy. Combine all these serendipitously. Dramatic results!

Expressionist portraits and figures are my specialty.

While sales are minimal, my feeling of accomplishment was and is great.

Four Websites

What the heck. The cost is tiny. I enlisted setup help from an American friend and pro photographer, Jacob Maentz—and built four websites using free, open-source software:

DaveWommack.com—My personal paintings, photographs and art.

Plus the three non-profit websites(websites explained later. See Volunteering): FineArtGalleryCebu.com, NatureCebu.com, and VolunteerCebu.com.

A sense of giving back and helping the locals. Quality websites. All told they took a solid three years of my spare time to build.

So I'm a big advocate of finding a hobby or interest, and developing it seriously. *No dilettantes needed.*

CHAPTER 14–ART

I'm an artist. An oil painter. Many subjects and genres, but my love is expressionist portraits and figures. I dwell in the recent past. With a few exceptions, modern, contemporary and installation art aren't my thing. My tastes run to realism and expressionism.

Maybe 25% of the time I copy outright or borrow ideas and pieces from another's art. It's a practice of even the greats. Almost all did it at first. Dates back hundreds of years. I don't apologize or disguise. If you're curious to buy, I'll tell you.

It constantly amazes me to walk into half the big Manhattan galleries and realize they couldn't pay me to put this junk on my walls. But it sells. Some buy for investment—at the recommendation of the gallery or their art advisors. Either I commend the salesmanship or condemn the flim-flam.

Good art deserves a good price. I don't apologize for my pricing. I like the painting. If you like it enough you'll pay my price. Otherwise I'm happy to keep it and enjoy it myself. Friends do get favored treatment, though.

Some art is different. I don't care for the result, but I can appreciate the artist's control of his medium/technique. Maybe a unique or very difficult process to execute. I'll give them a pass on my usual criteria for choosing or rejecting art.

Galleries are sometimes the artist's worst enemies. Yes, they can earn their 50% commissions by their sales and promotional efforts. They don't earn the right to cheat artists. But assuming all is on the up and up, they often promote boring repetition—wanting, insisting, year after year, to receive the same style/subjects/genre.

WOMMACK'S LIFE LESSONS LEARNED

"It's what the customer expects. It's what sells. It's what we can sell."

Sure, selling basically the same old thing—in its tenth recognizable reincarnation—is easier. But the artist is bored. *Bored silly.* Bored out of his mind. He wants to put out a fresh approach. And avoid being a one-trick pony.

CHAPTER 15–GROWING UP

Boy Scouts

My own experience with the Boy Scouts of America. And by inference others' experience with the Boys and Girls Clubs of America.

A heck of a lot of fun. Adult supervision. Safe. How else did I learn so much about nature? Earning merit badges. Advancing in rank.

Trees, flowers, animals, camping, maps and orienteering, survival skills, community service.

Summer Work

How the hell are you supposed to pick the right career, spend $100,000+ on education properly—if you don't have any idea what that career entails.

You talked to people who work there?

Yes. Somewhat helpful. *But not the real thing.*

The real thing is getting your hands dirty. Delving deeply. The day-to-day grind or exhilaration. *Before you actually try it, you don't know which.*

Different summers. Different experiences. All helped focus my mind on possible careers. Or conversely and just as important, identified careers I didn't want, couldn't stand.

Theft

I stole.

Gumball Toys

Age six. The temptation was too great. My eyes too wide.

Our next-door neighbor's job was to stock gumball machines with little toys encased in spherical plastic. His garage door unlocked to a treasure trove.

In my defense, I was shown them by my neighbor's son.

Mom caught me. A few dozen taken. I confessed. Had to return them.

Learned my lesson. *Almost.*

The Suit Drawing

As a teen, mom always took us to the annual sales at Hine-Bagby Clothier in downtown Winston-Salem, NC. It's where our family bought clothes, mostly on the sale dates.

About age twelve I connived with my brother, Dick, to stuff the "drawing" box (for a free suit). Of course we "won."

Somehow Mom sensed it. And we had to shamefacedly return to the store to "confess" our dastardly deed to the store manager.

Thank heavens our punishment didn't include the electric chair. Just a whipping and moralistic talking to.

Schooling

Valuable Courses

Richard J. Reynolds High School

English. Miss Hazel Stephenson, A.B. and A.M. and Miss Elizabeth Kapp, B.A.: grammar and literature.

Public Speaking. Mrs. Evelyn Garrison, B.A and M.E.: Debating. Defending either side of an argument. Memorization practice. Appreciation of quality magazines and newspapers to cite.

Mr. McLean Mitchell, B.S. and M.A.: World and United States history, arts and humanities.

Carnegie-Mellon University

Business Case Studies. À la the Harvard MBA program. I got a smattering here. Not nearly as thorough and intensive as the Harvard MBA program. That I would have relished.

Stern School of Business, New York University

MBA. Masters degree in Business Administration. A valuable degree. Almost a necessity nowadays. Brings a multitude of disciplines and perspectives to bear on the business of capitalism.

Looking back it seemed like a romp through bear-like greed, strangely devoid of ethics and compassion. Too bad. A dolop would have served the American public well in 2009.

Auditing Courses

For fun and profit.

Most schools allow it. Free—if you take a paid, full course-load.

Don't have to take tests, can buy or not the book, can read as little or much as time allows, can attend classes when possible, soak up the "extra" education, the lectures.

Outside your major. Culture. History. Art. Sociology. From stellar professors.

WOMMACK'S LIFE LESSONS LEARNED

Pack it in. Grab every advantage.

Free. Valued.

Theses

Almost worthless. Too easy to buy a good one. I never did.

Cut and paste from Google. Copy from texts. Plagiarism.

My paraphrasing. Maybe borderline/semi-plagiarism once in awhile. 98% original.

But the opposite is apparently too common now.

A better approach?

Write from any source. But be expected to defend it orally in class—from ripping inquiry, probing and critique. It'll ferret out your dearth of knowledge about someone else's ideas, someone else's construction.

Social Fraternities

Only serious ones accepted. Too much socializing is not what your parents are paying for.

Academics. And some socializing. Some athletics. OK.

After one year living in the dorm, I chose and pledged Sigma Alpha Epsilon Fraternity (SAE). Moved into the frat house with about thirty brothers.

One of my best decisions.

Many life-long friends came out of the fraternity. A good mix of careers in the SAE house: engineering, architecture, business, music, theatre, math. Enjoyed the variety immensely. Made for an interesting place.

Yes, beer parties about every 2nd weekend. I didn't drink and made it clear when I pledged that was non-negotiable—and I wasn't to be pressured to drink.

Over-Socializing

The bane of freshmen. Over-involvement in extra-curricular activities. Shunting school studies to second place.

Friends? Yes.

But make up your mind. Grades or socializing?

Your future or a wasted education opportunity.

CHAPTER 16–RETIREMENT

Retire before You Must

Our bodies wear out. Faster or slower. In part depending on the wear and tear we exert on them. Standing, running, heavy daily exercise, poor diet, marital and workplace stress—puts abnormal strain on body parts. Sooner or later the body rebels. Aches, headaches, sleep apnea, knees and hips that need replacement.

The temple breaks, crumbles, goes to dust—slowly, then faster. Then WHAM!

Retirement is Wonderful!

We retired age 53. My wife, Virginia, first. The stress of the Mount Sinai Hospital operating rooms was becoming too much. I would continue for another three years. Or so I thought.

Didn't happen. Luckily.

After Virginia retired. Three months later I told her it wasn't fun anymore. Getting up in the morning and going to work without her. So off to Cebu, where we could afford to retire ten years early at age 53. Besides, Virginia's pension wouldn't begin until two years hence, and our social security until twelve years hence. So we would be dependent on my earnings. Which barely covered the rent in our fancy Manhattan high-rise.

Luckily I decided to retire 6–9 months before the consulting job market seized up. After my last assignment I couldn't see an upcoming one—so we would be faced with no income and a large bill for monthly apartment rental. I'd be dipping daily into our meager savings. What nonsense is that?

So I retired too.

We gave our furniture away, packed our suitcases, ran down our security deposit, and slinked out of the apartment building to the airport.

24 hours later we were in the Philippines. Gone in a week!

Cebu, Philippines.

Cebu City, the second largest city in the country. Population about ¾ million. Relatively safe. Relatively.

In the Philippines we settled temporarily (for seven months) in Catmon, Cebu, staying in Virginia's sister's house. Her mother's house was about 50 feet away.

Plan A was to build a house on ½ acre of land in Tabogan, Cebu—2–3 hours driving time from Cebu City and about an hour from Catmon. It was nicely situated. Across the highway from a lovely cliff house lot. Virginia purchased it from a German lady. Afterward we let her live in her native house for another two years (since we weren't yet in the Philippines), until she moved to Spain. However, once we retired and came to the Philippines it quickly became apparent that the lot was way too far from the city for us.

Plan A ditched. On to Plan B: Find a lot closer. Buy and build.

Took a while, but we found a nice cliffside lot in Borbon, Cebu, 10 minutes from Catmon. 300 pesos per square meter. A real bargain.

Yet, near closing and after lengthy negotiations and investigations, it became apparent that there were substantial title issues. Issues which no one would guarantee to clear up as to cost or time.

About this time I became ill with kidney stones and had to be hospitalized for a few days. I poured out my misgivings about the whole direction of our search to Virginia. She was also coming to the same conclusion.

Plan B ditched. On to Plan C.

Rent a house in Cebu City. Nearer to what passed for culture and civilization—close to supermarkets and restaurants. Enlisted Elizabeth, Virginia's older sister and her husband Francis—both realtors—to search for us. After a month of duds we were getting quite discouraged. Then they steered us to Paradise Village, Banilad. The oldest subdivision in Cebu City, reasonably secure, about 110 homes, low structures, few walls, quiet, near all locations we wanted to frequent, and very affordable. 25,000 pesos per month in the home of Mrs. Almendras, a Cebu Provincial Board Member. Translated to about $600 per month at the time.

Signed.

Two-story, bright, safe, many bedrooms and a den, nicely landscaped, three levels of security. Mrs. Almendras turned out to be a very accommodating, undemanding landlord. Never raised the rent. Never bothered us. We liked her; she liked us. Nice situation.

What Will You Do?

Successful planning for early retirement isn't easy. Financial planning. Downsizing expenses and accommodations in advance. Building *serious* hobbies and side interests. Traveling while you can still walk and hike.

Consider a 5 to 10-year "temporary retirement" in a low-cost foreign country, prior to qualifying for Medicare at age 65.

It can be done. We did it.

Both Virginia and I retired age 53.

We moved to the Philippines and stayed for ten years. Low cost-of-living. New culture. New excitement. New hobbies.

After ten years we'd had enough. Returned to our favorite USA spot—San Diego. And waited two more years until Medicare kicked in.

You can too.

So what kept us busy in retirement?

Volunteering

I volunteer.

Sometimes volunteering directly:

SAPAK

Working with this boy's home/school/farm in Compostella, Cebu. Started and still run by an 85-year old Jesuit priest, Father Non. Home to 100+ boys. Our group, The Friends of SAPAK, donated free lunches, tuition scholarships, library books and bookcases, and dug clean-water wells.

Medical Missions

Helping with medical missions in the Philippines. Providing free examinations and medicine.

Each mission had of 3–8 doctors and about 10 nurses and helpers. Associated with the Diocese of Cebu which helped on weekly mission space downtown and transport.

Virginia played nurse (and I often tagged along and helped administratively). Around the Provence of Cebu. Our friends, Doctors Tino and Zenaida Froilan started it, collected millions of dollars in medicines on trips to the United States, brought the medicine back, and organized missions to various towns outside Cebu City.

Mission-for-Vision

Helping with my wife's personal charity in Cebu. Providing free reading glasses to poor, elderly mountain poor people.

Veterans' Village

Helping veterans (mostly United States Navy) write their resumes and practice for job interviews.

Costume Jewelry

My wife's hobby.

Virginia enjoyed making costume jewelry and her artistry showed. Very creative. Lots of time in the evenings spent putzing around with designs and tinkering.

Supplies were cheaply available in Cebu.

She gave hundreds of necklaces, earrings and bracelets to friends going to the United States to sell. Sales and profits were funneled back to her favorite charities in Cebu.

Sometimes volunteering indirectly:

Building Websites

I built three websites (in addition to DaveWommack.com, which showcases my personal art):

FineArtGalleryCebu.com

Highlights the works of Cebuano artists, of which there are many good one. Free to them. Maybe 75 artists. Purpose: to allow artists exposure and be able to sell their works direct without paying gallery commissions.

NatureCebu.com

The flora and fauna of Cebu. Names (English, Cebuano, Latin), text. 550 items. 1200+ photographs. Purpose: to facilitate nature teaching and foster an appreciation of nature.

VolunteerCebu.com

55 quality non-profit organizations in Cebu that need volunteers. Descriptions, their activities, along with current contact information. Purpose: to encourage volunteerism.

I identified an un-met need that I had an interest and talent for filling. Usually funded with my own money. Not too expensive. In this case using free open-source software and cheap website hosting. Costing $5 per month (aggregate for all websites) plus $12 per year for each domain registration). Not going to break the bank.

Then my spare time. Often in the evenings, at my desk, one eye on my computer—researching, Googling, typing—and my ears and other eye on the television. Three to four hours per night for three years built these websites.

Why?

Because I wanted to:

Give Cebuano artists more exposure and a way for them to sell their art directly. Thereby saving them from paying gallery commissions.

Create more awareness by Filipino and Cebuano students in nature. The value of saving the planet, preserving the ecology.

Get more people to volunteer with quality non-profit organizations. Doing good works. Allowing potential volunteers to quickly locate those organizations that could both benefit from their donation of time and expertise, and which also wanted and could properly manage volunteers.

Now, with one exception, I continue to pay the very small expense of web-hosting and maintenance. My "give back" to my wife's country, the Philippines.

And in San Diego?

All these projects are, of course, easier to do in retirement. Your time is freer, your schedule more flexible, your experience and expertise more helpful.

The only ingredient to add is determination. The old Chinese saying:

"The longest journey begins with a single step."

Take that step.

CHAPTER 17–RECOMMENDATIONS

Newspapers: *The New York Times*

Magazines: *The Economist, Forbes, Fortune, Readers Digest*

Political Websites: *Mother Jones, Huffington Post*

Poetry: 101 Famous Poems

Stock Brokerage and Mutual Funds: Vanguard, Charles Schwab

Stores: Target, Trader Joes, Lowes, B&H Photo, Best Buy, Apple Computer

Restaurant Chains: Chipotle Mexican, In-n-Out Burger, Jason's Deli

Other Websites: Google (Gmail, Maps, Chrome), Yahoo Finance, Arts and Letters Daily, PriceBlink

Software: Picasa, TurboTax, Quicken, Skype, Gallery 2, Open-Source, Microsoft Office

Communications: PhonePower.com

Cities: New York, San Diego, London, Hong-Kong, Sydney, Vienna, Paris

States: California, North Carolina, Utah, Oregon, Arizona, New Mexico

Countries: United States, Singapore, Ireland, Britain, Scotland, Australia, Malaysia

Plays & Movies: Gut-wrenching drama. Not fond of musicals, which are light of plot

Electronics: Apple Computer, Hewlett-Packard (printers)

Urban Parks: Balboa (San Diego), Central Park (Manhattan)

National Parks: Canyonlands, Yosemite, Sequoia, Zion, Grand Tetons, Hoa Forest, Olympic

Ports: San Diego, Sydney, Hong-Kong, New York

Castles and Mansions: Hearst's San Simeon, Biltmore House

Housing and Recreational Vehicles: Yurt, Prairie Style, Sprang, Scamp, Chinook Concourse

Cars: Volvo, Toyota, Fiat

Dogs: Doberman, Chihuahua/Jack Russell mix

Crossword Puzzles

Museums: Metropolitan Museum of Art, Whitney Museum of American Art, Cooper-Hewitt, Norton-Simon, Timken, Museum of Modern Art

Portrait Painters: Richard Schiele, David Leffel, Jacob Collins, Daniel Greene, Harley Brown, Ron Hicks, Lucien Freud, Rembrandt (van rijn), John Singer Sargent, Thomas Buechner, Jeremy Lipking

Portrait Photographers: Yousuf Karsh, Richard Avedon, Dorthea Lange, Bert Stern

Landscape Photographers: Eliot Porter, David Muench, Peter Lik, Galen Rowell, Ansel Adams

Cameras: Casio point and shoot; Sony, Nikon or Canon SLR's

Vests: Domke

Presidents: Washington, Lincoln, Teddy Roosevelt, Franklin Roosevelt, Truman, Carter, Reagan, Clinton, Obama

CHAPTER 18–OTHER BOOKS BY THE AUTHOR:

I have written eight books, all of which are available as e-books for $4.99 at www.Amazon.com and www.Smashwords.com. They are viewable as e-books on Kindle, iPad, & Nook, or Kindle Cloud through your internet browser, PC, or MAC.

Wommack's The Art of Parenting : Lessons from Parents and Mentors of Extraordinary Americans

Let's be honest. No other parenting books even try to show you how to make your son or daughter a great American.

We do.

Thirty (30) great men and women from across many professions, genders, politics, religions, and walks of life—the products of extraordinary parenting and mentoring.

This book offers the exact techniques, words, phrases, mantras —to propel your offspring to incredible success—toward rich, vivid lives. They worked for those parents and mentors. They can and will work for you too.

Mantras are the 21st Century way to lock your ideals, standards, ethics, and principles into formative minds. By definition they demand repetition. The phrasing may stay the same or almost the same. The stories, the elaboration, the background, the colors may bob and weave. But the cores of the mantras stay fixed. Stars to remember and guide one through life.

MANTRAS. The exact words used to motivate and guide those great future Americans. Distilled from over 500 biographies.

WOMMACK'S LIFE LESSONS LEARNED

These techniques, these words and phrases, WORK!

This book uniquely brings you the best parenting and mentoring advice. Straight up. No bull. The EXACT, SPECIFIC techniques and words the parents or mentors used to motivate their sons and daughters. To inspire them. Inspire them not just to succeed, but to rise above all others.

We present some of the smartest, most creative, most determined, most astute parents and mentors that ever lived. They threw their whole life into educating their children. Not in classroom ABC's and 3 R's. They educated their children in HOW TO LIVE LIFE.

The parents and mentors of:

Volume I: Kareem Abdul-Jabbar, Lance Armstrong, Warren Buffett, Julia Child, Elizabeth Edwards, Edward Kennedy, Sandra Day O'Connor, Ronald Reagan, Yvonne Thornton, Alice Walker, and Denzel Washington.

Volume II: Nancy Brinker, Hillary Clinton, Dwight Eisenhower, George Foreman, Andrew Grove, Quincy Jones, Wilma Mankiller, Paul Newman, George Soros, and Naomi Wolf

Volume III: Jane Pauley, Michael Bloomberg, Rachel Carson, Walt Disney, Ted Geisel (Dr. Seuss), Billy Graham, Steve Jobs, Michael Jordan, Barack Obama, and Paul Volcker

DAVID R. WOMMACK

Wommack's Vocabulary+ Buffet: Vocabulary, Word Usage & Pronunciation, Foreign Phrases, Quotations, Poems, Nursery Rhymes, Great Art/Artists, Architecture/Architects, Books/Authors, & Religions

Nothing thrusts your personality forward better than an expansive vocabulary—coupled with wit, an articulate delivery, cogent arguments, and an interest in & knowledge of the world. We can't address the latter—but *Wommack's Vocabulary+ Buffet* puts you easily on the road to a deep and dynamic vocabulary. Extremely helpful to creative writers too.

Our approach is vastly different from other tomes:
First—Portability. We're an e-book. Easily carried anywhere, consulted, studied.
Second—Pronunciation. Gone are the confusing accent marks & non-phonetic instructions. Our pronunciation guide is simple & phonetic.
Third—Illustrative sentences. We load you up with them—4 to 10 per word. Real help beyond definitions. Showing you how the various word meanings are correctly incorporated in sentences. Definitions alone won't fix your mind. Sentence usage will. No other vocabulary reference comes close to us—over 6,000 sentences for over 1,500 words.

Fourth—Games. We suggest a wealth of two-person & parlor games to reinforce your learning, allow you to practice in a competitive manner.
Plus—we include a body of extras to flavor your conversation:
—Quotations from Shakespeare's plays, famous poems, Dr. Seuss, Ben Franklin, Ralph Waldo Emerson, Henry David Thoreau, Will Rogers, the Talmud, Chinese proverbs, & nursery rhymes.
—Confusing words, prefixes & suffixes, & frequently misspelled words.

WOMMACK'S LIFE LESSONS LEARNED

—Common foreign phrases and expressions used in the English language: from romance & other European languages—plus Yiddish. A panoply of excitement.

—Useful tête-a-tête facts to have in your repertoire: great visual artists & their works, architects & architecture; classic books & their authors; major religions; Greek & Roman deities; state & country capitals; & the radio/military alphabet.

Wommack's American Adages and Aphorisms : That Propelled 20 Generations

Let me introduce you to my compendium of the 287 most used American Adages & Aphorisms. These are the sayings your mother and father used ad infinitum while you were growing up. Almost without your knowing it, they formulated words to live by, words to guide your thinking as you matured and throughout life. I have categorized them for easy reference. Adages such as:

* A clear conscience can bear any trouble
* Diligence is the mother of good luck
* Hope for the best and prepare for the worst
* If you lie down with dogs, you'll wake up with fleas
* You never know what you can do until you try

Hopefully they will prove useful to any reader who is a bit fuzzy on their definitions, or who want their children to learn the common adages.

To the newcomer to American literature, these will be fresh and exciting. I've provided somewhat irreverent meanings to help the reader along in understanding our culture.

To parents, this book will assist you in providing your children with a grounding in the meanings of America's favorite adages. And additionally, this book, along with your e-reader when taken on the road, provides an easy resource for family in-car quizzes—which will boost interest and enthusiasm during long trips.

Wommack's Self-Defense for Women : 3 Seconds to Live

Every woman (or girl) has a secret fear: THE FEAR THAT SHE WILL BE VICIOUSLY ATTACKED OR SEXUALLY HARASSED. It's a recurring nightmare. This book simplifies REAL SELF-DEFENSE FOR WOMEN!

Our guide is simple and straightforward. Not complicated. It can be learned—mentally & physically—and practiced at home or the gym. We teach you the techniques, in words and photographs. Clearly. Concisely. We discard many techniques that might be OK for trained karate or other martial arts experts, but are useless to you—and may even put you in more danger.

Variations of these techniques have been taught to thousands of his students by the co-author, Keiko Arroyo. They can and should be part of every woman's training.

The world is getting more and more dangerous. Be prepared!

Wommack's The Art of Leadership : Moving from Military to Industry

As a Captain, Lieutenant, Master Sergeant, Sergeant, or Petty Officer, YOU have more leadership ability than most managers.

This book has three purposes:

First, it teaches you how your military experience has prepared you to be a leader and successfully transfer those skills to an exciting career in the corporate world.

Second, it summarizes the best leadership practices of both the military and corporations, and

Third, it helps you find good employer prospects and wow them with your resume and interview skills.

It also helps you understand the winning ways of true leaders. Each aspect of quality leadership has its own chapter, with appropriate subheadings.

Wommack's Life Lessons Learned: Reflections in a Mirror

This book crystalizes the lessons learned during the 66-year lifetime of David R. Wommack. His professional career has spanned 7 realms—public and private accounting; sales & marketing of computer systems, software, & multimedia; restaurateur; financial consulting; an artist of expressionist portraits and figures; and now author and writer. He has lived in the United States, Vietnam, Indonesia, Singapore and the Philippines—and traveled to all the world's continents except Antarctica. Along the way he married, and he and his wife of 32 years adopted and raised a daughter.

Mr. Wommack writes in a pithy, staccato style that grabs and resonates in the mind. Pointed reminders of both the hard and glorious lessons learned. His style is delightfully succinct, humorous and without the trappings of literary pomposity.

Join in learning from his life conclusions, liberally sprinkled with tons of personal anecdotes.

Made in the USA
Columbia, SC
27 June 2024